The Singing Bowl

Journeys Through Inner Asia

Alistair Carr

CLOUDBURST MEDIA

First published in Great Britain by Cloudburst Media 2005
© Alistair Carr 2005

British Library Cataloguing in Publication Data ISBN:
0–9548611–0–8

Cover design: Oliver Hickey

Printed in Malta by Gutenberg Press
Set in 9/12.5 Stone serif by Pantek Arts Ltd Maidstone Kent

For Sarah

Acknowledgments

I would like to thank the following for their assistance and support: the Dukha, Jenya, A. Atai, Naraa, Tunga, N. Sanchir, Burmaa and all the Mongolian peoples who welcomed me into their world. A big thank you to Dr. Morten Pedersen and Alan Wheeler for letting me accompany them to, and through, the taiga, and to UB's ever friendly expat community, Laurenz and Anke Melchers, Hans and Pië Meulenkamp, Kim Wheeler, Graham Taylor, Alison Croft, Letticia, Michael Kohn, Andy Godwin and Christina Noble. And to John Thompson for being such a generous host on my very brief sejours in Beijing.

A thank you also to Dr. Angela Milner, J. Tito Sanchez, Tina Nimmo, Dr Christopher Chippindale, The Royal Geographical Society and The Scott Polar Research Institute for assisting and supplying research material. To Ben Maitland for critical assessments of early drafts. Heartfelt thanks to Grahame Sydney for his encouragement, to Dr Owen Marshall and writing his class of 2001 and to Anna Rogers, my ever patient editor, without whom this book might not have been posssible. A warm thank you to the late Johny Wilson whose support for my writing was, at the time, what a lighthouse is to a ship on a stormy night, and thanks also to Sir Peter Hutchinson, Dr David Munro, Shane Winser and the late Lorna Sage for their interest and help along the way. To Suzanne Ruthven, Guy Garfit, Oliver Hickey, Tony Mould and Cloudburst Media for guiding me through publishing conundrums.

I would also like to say a tender thank you to both my brother, Philip, for his steadfast support, and to my parents for their generosity, understanding and for providing such a wonderful home as Duchray and it surroundings to grow up in.

And finally to Sarah. I feel as if a star has floated out of the sky and is now walking by my side.

In memory of the 17,000 monks and 3,400 civilians who were executed in Mongolia between 1921 and 1941 under the Stalin Choibalsan regime.

This is a true story. Nounai is a fictional name.

Contents

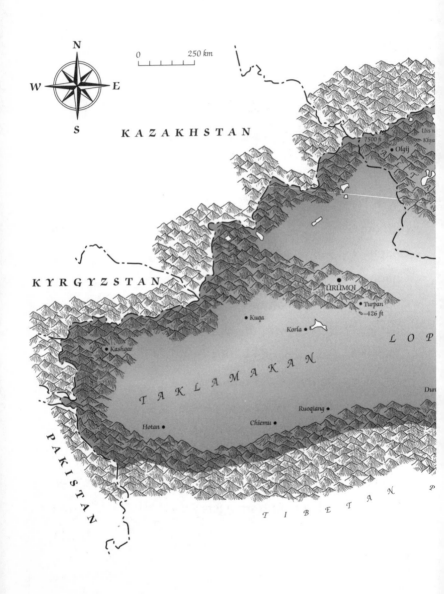

SIBERIA

7500 ft
Tsagaannuur
Ulaan Uul
Khövsgöl
nuur

Moron

nuur

rgas nuur

Kharus nuur

Khar nuur

Dorgon nuur

T H E

S T E P P E

ULAANBAATAR
4750 ft

M O N G O L I A

G O B I

Hami

huang

C H I N A

P L A T E A U

LANZHOU

Xiahe
9700 ft

XI'AN

List of Plates

All photographs taken by the author except where mentioned

Introduction

I woke up one ordinary day in London with a compulsion to leave for Mongolia. I knew nothing about the country, or even exactly where it was, but the sensation I felt was too strong to ignore. I never set out to write a book, but at the end of my wanderings, in a warm apartment in Ulaanbataar with a deel draped around my shoulders, I began to write notes from the often illegible travel diaries I had compiled. A year later, on a trip to New Zealand, I rented a small gas-powered hut by the sea, purchased an aging laptop, rigged it up to a car battery, took out my notes and started typing.

I thought I might find a career as a journalist in Canada, but when I visited the painter Grahame Sydney at his studio in Dunedin, he told me of a fiction writing course in Timaru tutored by short story writer Owen Marshall. A few days later, after scrapping my Canadian plans, I enrolled. Once again this book was set aside as I acquired the writer's toolkit and listened to my mentor's avuncular guidance. "Alistair," he once gently tendered, "Hemingway had what he called a 'shit detector'. I think you need one too."

Owen introduced me to Anna Rogers, his longstanding editor, and shortly afterwards I began to write the manu-script for this book while Anna patiently steered the helm. I then returned to the UK to experience a protracted bom-bardment of literary rejection and practical frustrations, some of which helped to mould the book to its current form.

I have not been back to Mongolia, but I hear it's changing. Where once there were only a few traffic lights and restaurants in Ulaanbaatar, now there is a plethora of both, the mobile phone is commonplace, tourism is growing, and the Dukha with whom I travelled are slowly having to leave the taiga, and totter precariously towards the long list of today's vanishing cultures.

**The Mill House, Belchamp Walter,
Suffolk — June 2004**

– Chapter 1 –

A nomadic capital

Smoke belches from the Trans-Mongolian engine. A paunchy Chinese man bares his brown teeth and spits a lump of shiny green phlegm onto the floor. Apparently satisfied with its viscosity, he slowly smears it around with his left shoe. Since leaving Beijing thirty-six hours ago, we've passed through Inner Mongolia, the Great Wall, the Gobi and into the vast steppe. The only thing I could translate in Beijing was the McDonald's logo and boarding the train was like a buffalo stampede, but now, between big-toothed smiles, I've come to an understanding with the twenty gawking Chinese in my carriage. They wanted to know why NATO was bombing Serbia. I explained with machine-gun and bombing noises, ending with an exaggerated grin. My squatting audience beamed back.

The steppe is like an ocean, Ulaanbaatar an island in its centre, encircled by a belt of gers. The naked eye can absorb this once communist, now capitalist city, and its surroundings in one short blink. The train pulls into the station, shunts to a stop, and the three Mongolians in my compartment collect their cardboard boxes and quietly disappear. I reach for my pack and step onto the platform.

"Accommodation?" a Mongolian woman asks. "I have rooms." I follow her to a car and the driver takes my pack. We drive to a bank and, looking out of the window to check that the car and my pack haven't disappeared, I exchange some dollars into some mutton-smelling tongruks. We drive into a courtyard and I'm given a small room in a flat. I find a bar, light a cigarette, point to a bottle of beer and sit outside contemplating my complete absence of contacts in this country.

Only a few months ago I awoke one morning in London with Mongolia imprinted in my mind, as clearly as the stars in a desert night sky. I was employed and had no plans to travel; nor had I read any articles or books about the country. Mongolia seemed absurdly incongruous, but possibly the only thing that made any sense at all. At twenty-eight I felt little, if any, connection with the life that had become mine. It was as if I had received a telegram that needed to be obeyed.

I organized a loan, exchanged my briefcase for a filofax, my suitcase for a blue rucksack, my shoes for a pair of hiking boots, my flat for a small green tent and my bed for a sleeping bag, and began to collect information on Mongolia and Inner Asia. It was a land of infinite unfenced space, felt homes and wandering nomads. On the back of a tatty brown A4 envelope, I spun a line that started in Ulaanbaatar, and wove south to the Gobi's dinosaurs, southwest to the lost settlements of the Taklamakan, north to the rock art sites of the Altai Mountains, east through the steppe's nomadic tribes and reindeer herders, before finally completing a neat circle back in Ulaanbaatar.

Now I'm here. Inhaling deeply on a Lucky Strike, I examine my surroundings where brown and black cows amble across the street opposite, and a grey horse trots past with a man wearing a burgundy deel and a hat that looks as if it's been bequeathed to him by an American settler. The square in front of me boasts a statue to a revolutionary hero and the parliament building looms like a tank. A sow and her litter trot along the pavement, but one of the piglets, presumably startled, runs into the tyre of a passing Jeep. It erupts into an hysterical morse code of squeals as it scrambles frenetically onto its side and disappears into a ditch, while mother and siblings, apparently uninterested, continue on their way.

As I cross the road to the British embassy, I see six lanes of traffic where there should be only four, all moving quite fast and headed towards me. Making myself as thin as possible, as if drawn up for an eighteenth-century pistol duel, I shut my eyes and feel side-view mirrors brush past to the cheering chorus of car horns. The man at the desk introduces himself as, "Andy Goodwin. Deputy Commissioner."

I explain that I'm going to be in Mongolia for a while and we look at the large map on the wall which shows a country the size of Western Europe, dotted with a few tiny towns. There are more horses than people.

"Are you looking for work?" he asks.

"No," I reply, "I'm just travelling. Can I leave a sketch of my route, just in case?"

"What?" he splutters politely, but uncomfortably. "So that if you disappear I say, 'There's a Brit missing in Mongolia'." He studies an area of green on the map.

"Something like that," I agree.

"How are you finding UB?"

I'm puzzled at first by the shorthand for Ulaanbaatar, but Andy explains and invites me for a drink on Friday evening.

The Steppe Inn at the British embassy is the expat's social anchor, where ambassadors and passing celebrities mix with Peace Corps and Volunteer Service Overseas workers. I need to get my visa extended and I'm introduced to Tunga who runs a small travel firm. I explain that I hope to see the dinosaurs in the Gobi and she tells me that she can set up a meeting with a 'dinosaur man'. She also says that she has an apartment for rent so I seize this offer, and a few days later I have my own untramelled space with a telephone, a bath and hot water.

My bedroom at home in Scotland is filled with stones, shells, animal and bird skulls, statuettes, feathers and coral. Wisteria tentacles through the window and dust hovers in shafts of light over books. At night bats dance around the outside light, like the shadows of brown trout rising and vanishing in a river pool. During the long summer holidays of my early schooldays, I would fish out the contents of our pond with a hand net and put everything from great diving beetles to newts into jars. Once I felt that I had sufficiently drained the pond's resources I would replace them. I would spend hours absorbed in books containing pictures of dinosaurs and prehistoric peoples and, as I turned each page, I would plunge into another existence. Perhaps I was fascinated because dinosaurs thrived for 163 million years and humans have prevailed for, at most, 400,000 years. Or maybe it was their peculiar forms, or the blood and gore associated with them. But whatever strange sensation dinosaurs inspire, I have never been able to shrug them off.

The Gobi was once a great inland sea. Now it's a barren place where the volume has been turned up on the silence. It's stuffed with remains of life from the Cretaceous, which was the bridge between ancient life forms and those that exist today. It was an aeon of dinosaurs and the nascency of placental mammals, which provided the stock for modern mammal groups like cats, cows and primates, as well as marsupial mammals like koalas and kangaroos. It saw the arrival of snakes, sharks, crocodiles, flowering plants, bees, wasps and ants.

The dinosaurs were extinguished 65 million years ago, possibly as a result of a meteorite that collided with the Caribbean coast off the Yucatan Peninsula, the net result being the catapulting into the atmosphere of billions of tons of rock and dust which blocked all sunlight. Others theorize that tectonic plate movements realigned the world's land masses causing the deterioration of favourable habitats. Although, oddly, the majority of land plant life appears to have survived, the dinosaurs were exterminated along with 87 per cent of planktonic marine flora and fauna. With these extinctions life diversified and evolved to dominate the earth as we know it today.

Tunga and I park outside the Institute of Palaeontology and walk into a small office where a woman is stationed behind a desk. Two dinosaur skulls sit on top of a cabinet behind her. Tunga says something and the woman shows us into a fusty boardroom where, seated at the far end, is a man with greying hair. We take chairs opposite him and he starts talking to Tunga.

"This is Barsbold," she says. "He asks what you want with a palaeontologist?" Barsbold is Mongolia's pre-eminent palaeontologist, responsible for the discovery of several species of Cretaceous dinosaurs.

I launch in, explaining that I've loved dinosaurs since I was a child and want to go to the Gobi. Tunga translates my monologue into a sentence. Barsbold looks at me without a flicker of facial movement, but with the air of a man who's survived communism in an institutional environment and spent a long time in the desert.

"He'll try and get you onto an expedition, but in case that doesn't work," Tunga says, "he's writing down his sons' details. They run a small tourist company." Nothing comes of that except that Barsbold's sons tell me that Steven Spielberg consulted their father for the dinosaurs used in *Jurassic Park*.

A week later I'm walking back from a restaurant with three travelling Danes when a stout policeman, flanked by two sturdy men wearing brown leather jackets, orders us off the street. "Passports," he demands. We hand them over. One of the Danes has left his behind in the hotel and the policeman slaps him across the face. "Money." He glowers, snatches the money from our hands and waves the book of cash in front of our faces.

He points into some shadows. "Police station. Come." I know that he's pointing away from the police station. The Danes and I stand still. Nothing is said, but we all know where this is going. The policeman says something in Mongolian and I imitate his words. He looks confused, consults his henchmen and returns our passports and money.

I recount this to Michael Khone, a New Yorker in his late twenties who's the editor for the *Mongol Messenger*. The floor of his office doubles as his bed and when he talks, in a voice that sounds wired, his eyes seem to get bigger, but in a crowd they move constantly, as if scanning for the next story. He tells me that the authorities have started arresting phoney policeman.

"Met the Mongolian president yesterday," he says. "He sat behind this huge desk. His bodyguard gave me his business card. 'President' was all it said." He looks edgy. "I know there's this scandal going on."

"Don't get murdered," I reply, only half-jokingly.

"That's what happened to an MP six months ago. They haven't found the killers, but this story could be great."

The president's black Mercedes drives past, preceded by the whirring sirens of a police car. Every pedestrian car is a potential taxi so I raise my right hand. A car draws up beside me, chauffeured by a man dressed in a suit, and we drive off. I want to have my own deel made and, having found an elderly seamstress, we drive through the ger district to the Black Market in search of fabrics. As the seamstress weaves through the crowd ahead of me, I feel a hand in my trouser pocket. Looking behind me I catch the sullen black eyes of a young man whose face is obscured by a white mask. He tugs his pilfering fingers away from my grasp, then almost jocularly slaps me on the back with the flat of his hand, before melting into the throng. I catch a glimpse of my companion and push my way to the fabric stalls. Nearby, a stocky Mongolian grips a man in a headlock and begins to smash his head against a pole, two women claw at each other's hair, and a woman in a brown deel raises her hand to reveal the head and skin of a snow leopard which she jingles about, as if it were a puppet.

When I return to my apartment I see outside the black outline of two dogs submerged in cluttered rubbish. A dim light glints across a pool of blood and on the stairs lie the prostrate figures of two adolescents. One of them groans as I fumble around in the dark for the keyhole. Once inside I flick the light switch but nothing happens. Feeling my way across the room, I sit down in an armchair, pick up a candle and push it into an empty wine bottle, before striking a match and turning on the radio. NATO has bombed the Chinese embassy in Belgrade.

The following morning the phone rings. "It's Burmaa, Tunga's niece. I've got a Danish anthropologist staying, Morten Pedersen. He wants to meet you."

"When?"

"He got in last night. He'll probably sleep for the next twenty-four hours."

It's been a month since I arrived and although I've got my visa extended, I'm increasingly frustrated with the problems of getting around this huge country. The tour operators are helpful but expensive and control tourists wanting to get into the wilderness. If I travelled with them I will be cheating and will feel cheated, for tourism and commerce are to nomads and their way of life what gangrene is to tissue. To be able to travel with scientists and see the real Mongolia before it disappears would be amazing.

The steppe is only half an hour's walk from the parliament building in UB. If I spend more than forty-eight hours in a metropolis I feel imprisoned and begin to petrify: when I lived in London I frequently escaped to Scotland's mountains. They seem so close – the dinosaurs, the nomads, the rock art and the reindeer people – but right now getting to them feels like trying to traverse an ocean without a boat.

I agree to meet Morten at Millie's, a small restaurant where the expat community gathers at lunchtime. I walk past a small crowd of Mongolians who are watching a fight between two young men, dressed in jackets. One of them collapses on the ground and draws himself up onto his knees, suggesting defeat, but his adversary swings his right foot, as if kicking a football, which slams into his jaw with a sickening crunch. The onlookers gasp.

I walk into Millie's where an unhealthily lean, thirty-year-old is sitting at a table devouring a hamburger. "Morten?"

"I've been dreaming of this hamburger," he replies. "And this milkshake."

"Where have you been?"

"Khovsgol. I've been living in a ger for the last six months." He chews vigorously.

"Cold?"

"Minus 45°," he answers.

"What were you doing?"

"Research. King's College, Cambridge."

Khovsgol is in northern Mongolia and borders Siberia. The reindeer herders live a nomadic life in Khovsgol's forest and tundra, known as the taiga. This is an opportunity too good to miss so I tell him about my plans.

"I'm returning to Khovsgol next week to stay with the reindeer herders, before spending the summer with my Mongolian family on the steppe." He orders another milkshake. "Usually travel alone. Do you want to come?"

"Yes," I answer. "Definitely."

Over the weekend I go for a walk outside UB with Hans and Pië, a Dutch and Danish couple, who work at Ernst & Young and the United Nations respectively. We park the car and climb over a fence, probably the only one in Mongolia, and head towards some hills. "There's a man shouting at us outside that ger," Pië says.

"Trespassing doesn't exist in Mongolia," Hans replies. "Let's go on."

"There are three of them and now they're all running after us."

We stop and wait for them. The patriarch walks past my companions without looking at them and stops in front of me. He leers, his face a furnace of aggression. His fists are clenched and he stinks of alcohol. Holding his left ear towards me, he slips his right hand into his pocket and takes out a rifle bullet, then points the tip of the bullet at my temple. He repeats the motion with renewed vigour and indicates the ger he's come from. His eyes are enraged, as if he wants a fight, but I remain silent. He simply points to the fence and replaces the bullet in his pocket. We walk back, feeling more irritated than rattled.

"Maybe this is a hunting ground," Pië says.

"Hmm," I mutter. "I rather got the impression that he wanted to shoot us."

The Mercury is a general food and grocery market, about the only place where you can acquire anything other than nomadic food. To avoid a visit here before embarking on an extended trip into the wilderness is as damaging to your well-being as holding a gun to your foot and pulling the trigger. There is nothing out there except goats, sheep, horses, yaks, camels, cattle and marmots, so meat is the big item on the menu though on a good day you may find a wild spring onion among the floating gristle. Morten and I pack a month's supplies into boxes and leave them in my apartment. We find a driver and a Jeep, and arrange to leave in two days' time.

– Chapter 2 –

Landlocked lobsters

Ulaanbaatar is small, as is the expat community, but at the weekends businessmen, anthropologists, diplomats, artists, adventurers, philanthropists and others often congregate in one of the few good restaurants. If I'm going to be sliding in and out of the wilderness, I need a social base so I decide to arrange a dinner party.

I was spared the horrors of modern baby mush, as I spent the first three years of my life in Africa where I thrived on a diet of avocados, shellfish and rice. My fondness for seafood has never left me: Neptune himself appointed me a subject of his kingdom when I crossed the equator on the HMS *Edinburgh* in 1973. But Mongolia is landlocked and it's impossible to find a mussel, let alone a lobster.

I speak to the best cook I know in UB, a German called Speckman, and we discuss a menu which I scratch onto a piece of a paper:

Coquilles St Jaques
Oysters
Seafood salad
Lobster (a whole one per person)
Chocolate soufflé
Cheese

Wines: Alsace, (Speckman's choice), Sancerre and Bordeaux Cru Bourgeois.

I tell him we're catering for fourteen. Speckman gets excited about the idea and his ponytail swishes in the air as he rings his contact in Beijing. "Yes. It can be done," he replies, with reliable Teutonic brevity.

"How much?" I ask.

"$100 per person including wine. A bottle per person."

I prepare some invitations and eleven expats and two Israeli travellers pay $100 each for the evening. Speckman triumphantly shows me fourteen crawling lobsters in the large fridge of his pub – they arrived on the Trans-Mongolian train from Beijing – and points to everything else on our list. Success.

He prepares a private, wood-panelled room in which the last Mongolian government agreed to resign. I like this touch: a feeling of history is invaluable. He garnishes the long table with a white cloth, cutlery, wine glasses, candles, wine buckets filled with ice, flowers and international flags plastered to the wall. The last touch is a trifle over-enthusiastic, but I'm not going to interfere. He's done magnificently.

As the evening begins an American merchant banker explains that he was staying at a hotel in Kazakhstan when the phone rang in his room. "Would you like a girl, brunette?" the receptionist enquired. He replied that he wouldn't. The phone rang again. "We have blondes and redheads?" He said that he wasn't interested and a rather confused voice asked, "We have boys if you wish?"

An American missionary describes how he was on a MIAT (the Mongolian national airline) plane that landed in the steppe. The pilot got out and began hitting the propeller with a large spanner. After a while he announced to the passengers that he would like them to get out and push the plane while he tried to start the engine.

This begins a cascade of disturbing stories about MIAT, an airline on which the UN simply won't let its employees travel. An American teacher recounts how she was boarding a plane to Khovsgol when a Mongolian couple asked if she could drop off their baby in Muron. There was a significant storm and the passengers looked scared. As she sat with this baby on her lap, two passengers knocked on the pilot's cabin door and suggested that it wasn't perhaps such a good idea to fly in this weather. The pilots examined the black skies and pelting rain, looked at each other and agreed that it was a bad idea to fly. They all disembarked and she returned the baby to its parents at the airport.

On another occasion a MIAT plane crashed, killing all on board. The subsequent inquiry discovered that the pilots had been drinking, but the authorities insisted that vodka was used only to clean the inside of the plane's windshield and this explained why there was alcohol in their bloodstream.

Tsaggan Sar is the Mongolian New Year and Morten tells how he was traveling from Beijing to UB on a MIAT aircraft piloted by two Chinese, but owing to bad weather the plane turned back just short of UB. The following morning the plane departed again, but this time with two Mongolian pilots. Mongolia was a whiteout and flying conditions were abysmal, but it was Tsaggan Sar and nothing could deter the pilots from participating in festivities. At 4750 feet UB is no flat field and as the plane descended into mountain peaks the intercom crackled into life as the pilots asked, "Has anyone got a mobile phone?" in Mongolian, Chinese and English. Apparently all the airport personnel were absent. No one had a mobile phone that worked, but hey, who cares, the pilots decided to land anyway.

After a conversation with a frustrated Dutch consultant who tells me that the cashmere privatization is on hold yet again, and a French anthropologist who recounts how a shaman apparently transmogrified into a bear, I turn to the US defence attaché and ask, "Are you planning to start a war? Or shall we talk about dinosaurs?"

"What are you really doing in Mongolia?"

"I woke up with the word Mongolia and came here."

"Yes, but why Mongolia?" He picks up a lobster claw as if it's a revolver. "What about the dinosaurs? Are you a palaeontologist?"

"No." I wipe my hands on a table napkin. "Are you going to start a war?"

Pië opens the door and looks horrified. "It's light outside," she exclaims. "Quick, let's go back in and get another drink." She weaves beneath me like an army in fast retreat and returns to the bar. In the masked blue shadows of dawn there is the random chatter of a bird and the silent step of an early morning Mongolian.

The next day, Morten and I pack our supplies into the driver's Jeep. "The driver's called Mixer," Morten says. "He doesn't know the way to Khosvgol."

Mixer looks at me, with a gentle smile. "*Sain bainuu,*" he says.

"*Sain bainuu,*" I reply, and he starts up the engine. "Is that a problem?"

"I remember part of the route and when we get lost we'll ask the nomads," Morten replies.

"How far is it?"

"Four, maybe five days."

I climb into the back seat among boxes and backpacks. The jeep moves out through UB's entrails, the city disappears and we are absorbed by the vastness of the flaky green steppe.

– Chapter 3 –

Steppe culture

We head slowly north for four days, driving past gers that lighthouse our path in clusters. The valleys are so wide they can't be walked across in a day. There are no roads, signposts, buildings, fences or trees – it's like driving across a field in a tractor. Generally the rutted tracks link up, even though they appear to disperse in opposing directions. Sometimes a track peters out, at which point we consult a compass or stop at a ger to ask directions.

A ger is a circular structure with a cone-shaped roof covered with layers of felt. The Mongolians have made gers their homes for hundreds of years as their design copes with the steppe's extreme weather conditions. A wooden lattice forms the walls and, at the top of the apex of the conical shaped roof there is a hole that allows smoke to escape. Gers are pitched wherever the nomads find pastures because they are not only simple to dismantle, but also light and strong; they are easily transported on the backs of yaks and camels. Once a Japanese consortium was commissioned to determine if the ger's design could be improved. After months of research they came to the conclusion that it could not be faulted.

I look across the mottled, green steppe which stretches into space and more space. "Mongolia," Morten pipes up, putting on a blue deel and wrapping an orange beuce around his waist. "Mongolia," he muses, "is first of all, inside us." He lights up a cigarette and expels a ball of smoke. Perhaps a country is a forum to explore one's personal geography and a magic magnetic pull exists between the individual and that country. As the wind tugs at my clothes I zip up the neck of my fleece and pull a deel around me. A black dog feeds off a rotting horse, its rib cage thrusting into the eggshell blue sky.

Ulaan Uul resembles the outbuildings of an early American cattle ranch. We park outside a wooden hut and a slender woman in her thirties with braided hair breaks into a huge smile, as we step inside. "My Mongolian 'mother'," Morten says, and slips into Mongolian. There are a few beds and some steps lead up to a stove, and beyond that two small doorways painted in coloured shadows. A ten-year-old boy with an impish grin sits on a window sill, casting for Morten's attention. Morten says something and the child feigns tears.

"What did you say to him?"

"I told Arambolt," Morten says, with a jester's twinkle, "that if he doesn't behave he'll be sent to boarding school in Denmark." Arambolt looks around and jumps out of the window.

We have the only vehicle in town. Nomads flock to our cameras and then gallop off. In a hut I locate the only telephone, a vast contraption with cords, plugs and holes. Seeing that I look sceptical about its viability, the operator stands up and indicates that I should write down the number. I shout my message and hear a whisper at the other end, immersed in a conundrum of crackle and static. I'm standing in 1999, holding a 1945 telephone, in a culture and way of life that predates Christianity. As I leave the hut I walk into a yak that's blocked the doorway.

The following morning eight Mongolians climb into our jeep and we drive to an ovoo, where there is a rumour of a ceremony sometime today. An ovoo is a cairn of stones which travellers circumambulate three times in a clockwise direction at the start of their journey. The skulls of favourite horses are placed on ovoos as a sign of respect for the dead animals. The term ovoo refers to the spirit master, or any other entity that is the object of worship. The promised event is a seasonal ritual directed by a lama where sacrificial meat is offered, distributed and eaten. The only hitch is that no one knows when the lama's arriving, or if he'll arrive at all.

Morten explains that ovoos are orientation marks which create fixed points of reference, anchored spots from which the totality of the environment can be apprehended and places where the nomads can loop into the infinity of the landscape. Imagine moving 360 degrees around an object, clockwise. If you look straight ahead you are part of the motion. If you turn your head to the left you fall out of the motion towards an infinite void, but if you look right as the nomads do when throwing stones at the ovoo, you fall into an inner and finite space, towards the very axis of your motion.

This ovoo is constructed from wood draped in blue ribbons and in its centre is a small grotto jewelled with gifts. Nomads in brightly coloured deels have gathered around the ovoo and more arrive by horse in twos and threes. Old women, their faces marked with deep, rugged lines like canyons and crevasses, leap off umber horses with paranormal agility. Time does not exist in the wilderness, only the day, the night and the sanctity of fire and water. Mongolians have survived on the reservoirs of their patience hewn from this harsh and remote land.

When the Buddhists arrive in a green Russian jeep Morten takes out a video camera. The lama climbs out, attired in a yellow uniform, and three monks get out of the back, resplendent in magenta robes. At the foot of the ovoo the lama constructs an altar of motley trinkets and tiny goblets, which he fills with incense as if pouring gold dust. A group of men with dark, weathered faces cut up a sheep's carcass and present it to the monks, who make it the mantelpiece of their shrine. The brain is balanced on a small branch next to a horse's skull.

The lama begins to chant, as do the monks, from scrolls inscribed with flowing script in brown ink. The small crowd of nomads are seated on the ground in a semicircle, as if they're listening to a speech. The cymbals are cacophonous, but the chanting is therapeutic as the soft, clumsy notes float into silence. The meat is distributed among the audience and the mantra continues, before shunting to a stop. A long blue ribbon like a rope is tied to the ovoo and everybody holds it as the lama says a blessing.

Arambolt takes my hand. We pass a saddled yak, cross a small river and head towards a ger where we've been invited to lunch. He talks as if telling me a combination of his troubles and thoughts. Finally, realising that I cannot speak Mongolian, he sighs, purses his lips and breaks into brisk song. I'm not sure if I'm holding his smudged hand, or if he's holding mine as we walk across the grazed, verdant steppe which is littered with dung and bones. We sit down, and I remove a photograph of a whale from my pocket.

"Whale."

"Whall," he replies.

"Yes ... Nearly."

"Ger." He points to one and picks up a couple of stones.

"Ger," I reply. His logic is more adroit than mine.

It's customary to arm yourself with stones when approaching a ger. Dogs are to gers what the crow's nest was to ships, but with the additional responsibility of security. Some of these dogs are killers. We stop outside the ger's tiny, painted wooden door and Arambolt skips in. I bend down and step inside. Movement in Mongolia is always executed in a clockwise direction: inside a ger, walking around an ovoo, passing food or drink, even dressing. A half-naked child stares at my knees, and slowly works his way up until his eyes reach mine, almost bending over backwards on the balls of his heels. He balances himself, giggles and scampers outside. I work my way round to Morten and nod at my host, "*Sain bainuu.*"

"*Sain bainuu.*" The facial wrinkles are so deep they look like unattended scars and his eyes sparkle like polished crystals.

"*Sain ta,*" I reply. When he smiles at me, his eye lines twirl into the sides of his head.

I sit down cross-legged on the floor, since it's impolite to point the soles of your shoes towards another person. Because we are in a circle sitting positions are limited. Our host is seated at the top centre, with Morten and I on one side and his family on the other. Around the ger walls are beds and two painted chests of drawers, one adorned with a postcard of the Dalai Lama, the other with a picture of a crucifix. There is an area for cooking utensils, another for shoes and other things. No space is wasted and the possessions are meticulously arranged.

The Mongolians are beautifully dressed and lead their lives with order, tradition, dignity and discipline. The older children look after the younger and there is a presence of soft, spontaneous laughter. It's the happiness, generosity, integrity and resilience of these nomads that I feel so comfortable with. Everything appears unconditional, part of a natural affinity of being. They have a peaceful, observant quality, as if they are a part of the wilderness and the wilderness is a part of them.

Our hostess, a curvaceous woman with high cheekbones and brown eyes, hands me a bowl of dried meat, gristle and noodle soup. One of her daughters carries a churn of water with fingers of ice tapping against the sides. A kid goat bounces nimbly through the doorway but is ushered out by one of the children. The fire is fuelled by animal dung and the grass floor is laid with clotted cream (seasonal), bread, yak's cheese and vodka. Mongolian food is digestive cement. My hostess reaches for my bowl to refill it and, as I'm about to cover it with my hand, Morten intervenes with something between a laugh and a whisper: "You've got to have at least two bowls. It's polite."

I give her my bowl and spread some clotted cream over a slice of hard bread. More milk tea and the afternoon slides away; then it's time for toasts – in vodka. These start as a trickle and settle into a flood. The communal cup is downed on each occasion and then passed on to the next person. I'm slightly drunk and I smile at everyone, because everyone's smiling. I bend down and out of the cosy felt home and look up at the night sky, as a deep roar resonates from the direction of a silhouetted copse.

The next day we drive through undulating valleys freckled with ancient burial mounds and arrive at Tsaggan Nuur, an assortment of huts marking the end of the road. In the local shop all that is displayed on the shelves are single rifle bullets and three loaves of stale bread. On the other side of the river, fortress-like mountains signal the end of the steppe and the beginning of the taiga.

We walk into a long hut and Morten hands a note of introduction from his family in Ulaan Uul to a man in his late thirties with groomed black hair. The man nods his head and leads us into a bare room, decorated with a warped, wooden table and some canvas sacks. "We can stay here," Morten says. "I told him we're going on to the Dukha reindeer herders. He knows someone who can take us to their summer camp." Morten tells me that he spent a month with the Dukha last winter, and that they move camp several times during a year in search of lichen pastures.

In a capacious, but sparsely furnished room, a young woman with a sleek figure and oily black hair tied into a loose bun, is bent over a stove. Two rugged, elderly women with wizened faces and necks like plucked pheasants sit either side of a wooden crate drinking milk tea. Not a silver grey hair is askew, and it's as if their deels have been ironed around their bodies. One of them asks Morten a question. She looks shaken at his reply and says something.

"What did you say?"

"I said that we're off to the reindeer herders," Morten smiles. "She said that they're wild and dangerous, and that we shouldn't go." The woman's shrivelled facial lines seem unusually taut and she sucks on her bottom lip, as if unconvinced. She sits with her hands on her knees, her eyes full of concern. A short man with a large, puce birth mark on his right cheek walks into the room. He speaks to Morten briefly, then leaves. "The Dukha are 40 miles away," Morten says. "He knows where they are and will meet us at ten tomorrow morning. He's bringing horses."

We pack our primary equipment into three blue waterproof sacks and make eight goody bags for the Dukha consisting of sweets, candles, knives and flour. "How long will we be away?" I ask.

"Two weeks, maybe more."

"And food?"

"There'll be meat there." Morten packs away two packets of spaghetti, four Russian tins of sardines and three onions. "We need to travel light."

"Shouldn't we take more?" I enquire anxiously.

"No." He ties a length of white string into a tight knot around the top of a sack.

The following morning Mixer drives us to the river where Morten tells him that we'll be back in three weeks and to wait for us in Tsaggan Nuur. Unperturbed at this prospect Mixer drives off over the brow of a hillock. A chain links the banks of the river and attached to it on the other side is a semi-submerged raft made up of planks of wood tied to diesel drums. A man pulls himself along the chain to the 'ferry' and brings it over. Timetables and deadlines are incongruous in this wilderness culture: three hours behind schedule, a ball of dust appears in the distance. I remove my binoculars and can make out six horses, our guide's crimson deel and one other rider.

The horses – actually they're Mongolian ponies – jerk to an abrupt halt beside us. Their nostrils flare and their eyes roll to the sky as they jump onto the raft. We climb on and sit down in the middle, squashed among ponies' legs and our gear. The ferryman pulls us to the other side of the river, and our sacks are roped onto the back of a pack-animal.

I am not designed for Mongolian ponies. Mongolians hover around 5 feet or under; I'm well over 6 feet, a giant in a land where nature has crafted life to be small and hardy. Even with the additional hole that I puncture into the goat-skin stirrups at the end of their length, they are too short. I climb onto my rufous pony and adopt a position usually reserved for steeplechase jockeys. Laden with our gear, Morten, the guide and I trot off across the steppe towards the taiga.

The peaks are dusted with snow, and the rocky outcrops look like the ruins of medieval castles traced against a brilliant blue sky. For hours we ride past herds of horses and isolated gers. Then we descend into a narrow gully and climb out the other side into the company of four mounted herdsmen. Our guide talks to a man in his late fifties who appears to be the leader of this small group. His perched position in the saddle, slightly hunched shoulders, clenched left hand and slow head movements, imply significant pain.

Morten sits alertly and speaks to him in Mongolian with tones of reverence. "He's the Dukha's leader," Morten says. "He's been ill for months and has come out of the taiga to see the doctor in Tsaggan Nuur. He was complimenting me on my Mongolian. The last time I saw him I couldn't speak a word." The herdsmen walk down into the gully and we trot away. "If he's that ill," Morten grimaces, "he probably won't make it back to the taiga."

The mountains encircle us as we get closer to the taiga and the light fades into dusky blue. Since I was a teenager I have suffered from a back complaint, something about a weak lumbar vertebra, and riding this pony is an exercise in prolonged discomfort. I just hope that my back doesn't go into spasm. We stop outside a ger at the edge of the taiga, where possessions are stacked on the grass outside. We dismount, remove the saddles and tether the ponies to a pole.

"They only arrived a few hours ago," Morten says, removing his head torch from one of our sacks. "During the winter it gets so cold," he continues, unrolling his sleeping bag, "that wolves club together in packs to go hunting. Last winter a pack numbering seventy was sighted."

Ger life starts before dawn. Armed with only their body clocks, which do not revolve around the hands of a watch, the Mongolians live according to the shadow of the sky, the sun's angle and the pitch of a dog's bark. This culture ensures that any traveller is welcome for a while but stipulates an interrupted night's rest as social calls start around five. My eyes feel puffy and I roll over in my sleeping bag as two herdsmen walk in. Our hostess offers them milk tea and noodle soup, then quietly waits on them in between other early morning chores. I fall asleep and awake to our guide trying to rouse Morten, who sits up, scratches his head and looks at his watch.

"What is it?" I grumble.

"Mongolians," he mumbles. "He said that it must be midday and that if we're going to arrive at the Dukha's camp by nightfall, we should leave."

"What time is it?"

"Seven."

Rising late in the summer is as vulgar as rising early in the winter, and I stroll into the ambient, honey light, pour some water into a cooking pot and shave. A can has been put up against a small cardboard box as a firing target. Some distance away two men are standing behind a third, who's sitting on the ground holding a rifle. He's wearing a pair of round-rimmed glasses and the left lens is cracked. I walk over and am invited to have a shot. I lie on my stomach, dig my elbows into the ground and pull the rifle butt into my shoulder. I aim at the target, squeeze the trigger and a match box flips into the air above the can. I didn't even know it was there, but it was the target, not the can. The three men look at me, stunned, somewhere between awe and misgiving, as if they've sensed that something's not quite right. I turn to them, ask, "Is that all right?" and, before they have a chance of offering me a second shot, I return the rifle.

My pony tries to detach himself from the post as I walk towards him. My host, a middle-aged man, his face furnished with furrows and grooves, comes up to me, smiles and jabbers to Morten who translates, looking bemused. "He says that he fears and respects you. Not only are you very tall, but you're an excellent shot."

We mount up. A garrulous fourth man, a local merchant who sells flour to the Dukha in exchange for velvet antlers, joins us with his packhorse. We canter across the last of the steppe's pebbles, bones and blades of grass, before pulling the ponies into a walk at the taiga's edge. It's like arriving in another country as we step into the canopied foliage and ride through the panoply of greens, along corridors of trees and up into the mountains.

– Chapter 4 –

Travels with the Dukha

I tie the collar attachments of my deel and bow my head half-mast into the pony's mane as it begins to snow, and then stops, almost as suddenly as it began. In the dappling light of fluorescent lime larches, moss becomes a river of liquid gold. We walk through illuminated trees and a tundra that is sprinkled with small purple and orange flowers. The white mountain summits are enveloped in curling clouds. My pony and the packhorse in front sometimes flounder up to their knees, scrambling for a footing in the waterlogged fields of moss. We arrive at the saddle of a mountain pass and the cold wind pinches my face with uncut fingernails.

Larch trees slide into the valley below us which is veined with a spindly river and straddled by seven small white tepees. Tiny people, dogs, reindeer and horses move like coloured speckles around white cones. The dogs scent a disturbance and bark at snapping branches as our small cavalcade begins its descent.

As our ponies walk into the fringes of the camp, snarling, white Siberian dogs prowl towards us. Reindeer lie around the tepees and barefooted children stare with questioning black eyes. We stop outside the open canvas entrance of a tepee. I force my legs to reposition themselves from the triangles they've formed and dismount. A man with thick, tangled black hair sits on a brown horse studying me. He supports a small boy on the nape of the horse's neck and is smoking a hand-crafted pipe. He says something without taking his eyes off me.

"What did he say?" I ask.

Morten grins. "He said you have a good body."

The man continues to stare, his face devoid of emotion, and blows a stream of smoke through pouted lips. The Dukha seem pleased to see Morten. Their tepee, or otrs, is about 9 feet high. It's constructed by stretching dressed reindeer hides over the skeleton of up to twenty poles, all slanted towards a central point. These are tied together a short distance from the top and an adjustable flap is left open to allow smoke out through the stove pipe.

I stoop down and follow Morten through a flap at the bottom which serves as a doorway. He introduces me to the weathered patriarch, Gambat, who's sitting cross-legged on the floor, puffing on a wooden pipe and sharpening a knife. "Alstar," he pronounces with some verve and gabbles a sentence. "He says you have a good name. It means shaman's blessing," Morten says, as I nudge a rifle to one side and lean against a wolf skin.

A reindeer peers in through the doorway, its velvet antlers like woollen coral, and it feels as if I'm touching the world with new fingers. Gambat's wife offers us a bowl of reindeer milk tea, cheese and bread. She moves about the stove and us like a butterfly around a rose bush, as if we were part of her family. Small strips of black meat are draped over a pole and possessions are neatly stacked or piled around the dwelling's circumference. Like the steppe nomads, the Dukha live in round constructions. Their internal layout is similar and rules govern the way they move inside.

A man in his thirties with the frame of a ferret, blue eyes and a coating of ginger hair that expands down his cheeks into a curling beard, steps into the otrs. "Heeeeeey," he says in an American accent.

"Hey man." Morten shakes his hand. "This is Alistair, Alan Wheeler. When did you arrive?"

"A week ago," Alan replies. "They're moving camp. How long did it take you to get here?"

"We left Tsaggan Nuur yesterday morning. When are they moving?"

"Soon, that's all I know. Everything all right with the permits?"

"The mayor wanted more money. He was drunk, threatened to come back and tripped over the doorstep on his way out. We left before he returned."

Alan Wheeler, from Oklahoma, is thirty years old and has been living in Mongolia with his wife, Kim, for the last five years. He worked as a teacher in the Altai Mountains and is now an anthropologist, fluent in Mongolian and Tuvan. When he was back in the United States, he decided to marry Kim after seeing her perform a perfect swan dive into the sea at night. He'd never met her before and a few months later they were man and wife. They arrived in Mongolia in the days when food was acquired with ration tickets and people formed long queues in UB to get their quota.

The Dukha are animist nomads, their travel determined by their need to find lichen pastures for the reindeer and by the availability of game to hunt. They move many times during the year and usually cover great distances in doing so. The term Dukha probably derives from Tuva, a region in Russia that borders north-western Mongolia. Thirty-six Dukha families live in the taiga, seventeen in the east and nineteen in the west. The latter area was settled during the 1940s so the Dukha could avoid being drafted into the Soviet army, whereas the eastern Dukha have made this place their home for a couple of centuries.

In 1956 the government established a fishery in Tsaggan Nuur and because of the hardships of nomadic life, many of the younger Dukha moved to work on it. In 1972 the government encouraged the Dukha to hunt sable for their pelts and provided them with guns, ammunition and salaries. But by 1985 reindeer numbers had fallen alarmingly, to under

700, so the government imported 50 reindeer from Tuva to replenish stock and in 5 years the herd swelled to 1200.

With Mongolia facing economic crisis in 1992, the government could no longer afford to pay salaries to the Dukha and decided to lease them the reindeer. Since then herd numbers have plummeted. The fishery became defunct, as a result of over-exploitation in the new found freedoms of a market economy, and many of the Dukha returned to the taiga. With both hunting and salaries gone, there aren't enough reindeer to sustain the Dukha already in the taiga and those returning to it. The Dukha harvest the velvet antlers in exchange for flour and other goods, but this affects the reindeer's immune system and, combined with inbreeding, the herd's health is declining. There is little wildlife to supplement the Dukha's diet of reindeer meat.

"You said there would be meat here," I say.

"There isn't. Sorry," Morten replies.

"We have some sardines and two packets of spaghetti for how long – two weeks?"

"Milk tea, bread and sugar it is," he answers, in the tones of a hardened scientific expeditioner.

"I think I've got giardia," I mutter.

"How many times are you going?"

"About four times a day."

"You're getting there," he says, smiling.

Giardia is an unfriendly parasite that dissolves the contents of the stomach into yellow porridge and removes the safety catch. Stomach problems are no joke in the wilderness, especially constipation. The waste piles up inside you and starts to rot. Within a certain time you need help. Giardia, although inconvenient, is not life-threateningly pernicious. You just lose a lot of weight.

The reindeer leave and return to the camp at specific times during the day with no human interference or encouragement, making a noise between a toad's croak and a dog's growl. I slide onto the back of a saddled reindeer and pursue the course of the quiet river around a contorted bend, as a gentle breeze shuffles through the undergrowth and the otrs disappear behind us. My legs dangle, almost scraping the top of the lime-coloured moss and pastel-green lichen. Enfolded in my deel I ride around the land of tepee nomads under the softly tinted lips of long extinct volcanoes. I drift up the valley towards another Dukha camp, to the clicking melody of reindeer hind legs, my view framed by velvet antlers.

I am chorused by the mellifluous laughter of children racing past on reindeer and I hear the elastic strumming of their mounts; dogs dart through the tundra. In the shadows born of setting sunlight, an eagle glides down the valley and Bartulluch, a portly man, rides up alongside. He gives me a Mongolian lesson by pointing to objects around us and, depending on the quality of my mimicking, smiles, shakes his head or frowns.

A week later, I look at the world from the worm-like sanctuary of my tent, wrapped in the cocoon of my goose-feather sleeping bag. The inside of the tent is frozen. My deel, an insulator against wind-chill during the day, assumes the role of blanket at night. My watch was stolen in UB and I've learnt to tell the approximate time by the sun's position. The camp is moving. Some of the otrs have been taken down and those still standing are being dismantled. Possessions are packed into reindeer skins which are evenly weighted and strapped to the sides of the reindeer. There is a feeling of unity and efficiency – each individual has a role to play. There are 175 reindeer: 45 are loaded up with possessions and a further 11 have been saddled up as mounts.

The smaller children are hoisted onto the back of the animal, cushioned between nomadic possessions. I pull myself onto the saddle, as Morten rides up and removes some tobacco from a pouch hidden in the waist of his deel. He rolls two cigarettes, gives one to me, then tucks his head into the collar of his deel and, shielding it from the wind, lights up. "There was this missionary," he says, "who came here and gave them all Bibles. They thought she was great."

"Why?"

"They could roll thousands of cigarettes from the pages," Morten replies, making no attempt to disguise a huge grin.

"I've started rolling with newspaper and Russian pipe tobacco, and I'm failing," I say. "The newspaper we left by the fire last night had gone this morning."

"They leave nothing to waste."

"It's incredible the resemblance they have to the native American Indians," Alan says.

"One theory suggests," Morten adds, "that the American Indians came from Inner Asia, moved across Siberia, over the Bering Strait and into Alaska."

"When one of the Dukha die," Alan continues, "the body is carried underneath the back of the otrs, so the spirit can't find its way back. And when the husband returns from hunting, even if he's been away for a month and arrives empty-handed, which isn't uncommon, he's greeted by his family as if he's only been away for a few hours." With no announcement or address the Dukha move off in a linear caravan. "Anthropology," he adds, "is really travel writing without the room service." Alan kicks his heels into the pony's flanks and trots off.

In four hours seven families have packed up their lives, leaving no sign of having been there. A reindeer drifts past, on its back an infant blanketed in a basket and cradled in a saddle. I follow the long, wandering line as the herd is ushered up the valley by a crescent of mounted children behind us. On the other side of the mountains is Siberia.

Early explorers discovered mammoth carcasses sticking out of the icy banks of the River Lena and their remains have been found throughout Siberia between the Gulf of Ob and Wrangel Island, west of the Bering Strait. By the Middle Ages people thought that the curved mammoth tusks belonged to the fabled unicorn and, in China, the mammoth was called 'the hidden mouse' or the 'mother of mice'. The Manchus referred to it as the 'ice-rat'. The first emperor of the Manchu dynasty, K'ang-hi, writes in his book on the animal world: "Far in the north in the land of the Russians, these rats, as large as elephants, live in the ground. When air, or sunlight touches them, they die instantly ... The flesh of this animal is ice-cold and very efficacious in fevers. Their teeth are like those of elephants and the people of the north make vessels, combs and knife-handles out of them."

The mammoth was incorporated into the folklore of the Siberian Yakuts who were mystified as to how these huge carcasses appeared on the banks of the lakes and rivers. They presumed that these giants must have lived in the depths of the earth, or under water. Their name for them, Ukyla, translates as 'water animal'. There are accounts of nineteenth-century travellers sawing off mammoth limbs and cooking them, and a Mongolian Khan had a throne sculpted from mammoth's tusks.

"I remember when I was on an expedition in Siberia," Morten says, "hearing the bears scratching around outside my tent at night."

"Did they bother you?" I ask.

"Our guide shot one. He emptied about twenty rounds into its heart. You've got to be careful with bears – they can still kill when they're mortally wounded."

The caravan is spread over a couple of miles. Groups of reindeer linked by rope, tail to head and head to tail, vanish into the choppy mountain scenery, and then reappear. The body of the herd is managed by women and children, some of whom carry larch branches to brush the animals along. The men pick up escapees in the rear. Herding isn't as easy as it looks and after I'm outwitted by several calves I study the tactics of a professional, and watch a child.

"The reason I became an anthropologist," Morten says, "is because it was described to me as 'philosophy with people in it'." He goes on to explain that the Dukha's perception of environment is closely connected to vision and that Mongolia's nomadic peoples have come to despise spatial confinement. When he tells them about Denmark, its size and number of inhabitants, they look terrified and picture a people who must constantly avoid bumping into each other. The Dukha highlight places at the expense of spaces.

We climb up through a mountain pass and I notice an owl has been carved into a tree, presumably by one of the Dukha. Morten continues, with academic eloquence, "When they move, they not only move their belongings, but also their sense of belonging." I see what looks like a chopping board on the ground and pass it by, thinking that it may have been discarded. "Can you imagine how a New Yorker would cope with being instantly transported to the steppe?" Morten asks. "Or a Mongolian transported to Manhattan?"

"The Mongolian would fare better," I reply.

The reindeer people have gathered in a gorge and seeing the chopping board I ignored being handed to a smiling face, I feel ashamed.

"You know what the Dukha are calling you?" Morten says.

"No?"

"Undurgongor."

"What?"

"About a hundred years ago there was a Mongolian who was so tall, he could stick his head out of the top of a ger."

The group moves off under pastel-coloured volcanoes onto ancient lava flows stitched with snow. It feels like I'm sailing in velvet, as I squint in the reflection of the snow and pass through a canyon seeded with a small ovoo. I pull away from my self-imposed herding duties. With no evidence of life ahead, or behind, my pony screams for reassurance. A small urn with a peanut-coloured teddy bear has fallen to the ground. A chopping board is one thing; a teddy bear in distress is another altogether. I dismount, pick up the urn and lead my pony through the tundra.

A shout in front shatters the cold, still air. One of the baggage reindeer has slipped and the saddle has pinned the animal's head to the ground. It belongs to Ombon, a man who earlier gave me a wolf's ankle bone for luck. The fall has sliced a small trench into one of the antlers and a thread of blood dribbles to the ground. One of his children takes my pony, as Ombon and I remove the saddle. The reindeer staggers to its feet, panting heavily, and the underside of its rubbery, grey tongue is stuck with bits of moss and lichen.

In the fading light there are two long, pink clouds like stockings. The caravan is gathering at the top of a small hill snuggled at 7500 feet. We're stopping for the night and the children set up mini otrs, as fires are lit and I'm offered a bowl of milk tea. It has taken six hours to travel a little over 12 miles.

In the morning I wake to find the children have collected the herd, which has been grazing in the valley below, and the Dukha are packing up their makeshift camp. I mount my pony as the Dukha trickle away and settle alongside the abdomen of the convoy. From the bottom of a steep mountainside, I watch the caravan snake its way up in one long line to become silhouettes stencilled into a deep, blue sky. At the mountain's crest the herd pummels the snow, before beginning the long trek down. I slide off my pony. With his ears pricked forward, he gingerly follows me down the tightly congested contours, sometimes losing a footing on the scree. In the sunlight, the rising steam from his shoulders looks like smoke from a kindled pile of dewy autumn leaves.

Sparklers of small white, purple and yellow flowers light up our invisible path, before exploding into knee-high grasses and bushes of wild rhubarb. The air is redolent of wild flowers, warm grass and pony sweat. I select a position behind a horse carrying a boy of maybe ten, who's singing.

He has a rifle strapped to his back and, following the line of the muzzle, I look up at the sun which is ringed with an enormous halo.

On the reindeer in front, a young girl holds a brightly coloured bouquet of flowers in the hand of her outstretched right arm. Her small body sways in rhythm with the gentle swell of her transport. In the saucer of the valley ahead, the reindeer people are coming to a stop. This will be their new home and mine, for a while at least. Within a few hours the camp is up, as if it's always been there under the folds of mauve mountains.

On a mountain ridge two eagles soar above the camp. I get up in the evening twilight, stretch my arms and mirror their movements on the thermals. They circle closer and closer, until one of them almost touches me. Two more eagles glide towards us and join our dance.

"I wouldn't mind a hamburger," Morten says. "You can light a fire with the end of a cigarette by putting it inside dry dung." He adds, "Mongolians often use urine on open wounds as a disinfectant. It's not uncommon to see a Mongolian pissing on a horse's leg."

"The Dukha believe that if you hold a bear's claw over a woman's breast, it ensures that the woman's milk is good," Alan says. "I'd really like to spend a year living with these guys. My wife's ..."

"You're a father," Morten interrupts, "with another on the way." He rolls a cigarette out of newspaper and under the theatre of a billion stars, Alan breaks into the lyrics of a haunting Mongolian tune.

I wake up. It's cold. There's snow on the tent. Children are laughing and I can hear them running through the powder, enjoying the tingling impulse of feeling alive. The air in the tent is stale and I peer outside my stuffy husk, breathing the freezing mountain air; a reindeer sticks its nose into my doorway. Morten and I are leaving so I pack my gear and one of the Dukha packs our horses. The camp collects to see us off and Gambat and two other herders join us on our return journey to Tsagaan Nuur, 40 miles over the mountains.

I tie up my deel, pull my hat down and we trot along one valley, into another. White mountains are stamped against a Mediterranean blue sky. Plants are frozen and the ponies billow a heavy mist to the muted thud of hooves on snow. It feels if we're walking through winter. The steppe beyond the mountains is a pine-green sea. Gambat peels away from our group and wanders into the wilderness, apparently off to visit a friend. Giardia is eating away at me and I have replaced my belt with a piece of string, which is loosely wrapped around my protruding pelvic bones. We descend out of winter into spring. My pony's ears frame stubborn snow patches, midget trees and moorland tundra. The taiga ends.

The steppe quivers in the warm light, resonating like the last hum from a singing bowl, and gers resemble yachts sailing along the horizon. At 4500 feet, it's as if they're a symbol of another planet and another season – summer. The five of us form a line, as if preparing for a cavalry charge, and with a quick "Hhaaaa" we thunder across the steppe, galloping past scattered herds of wandering horses and vultures bickering over a carcass.

A scrawny border guard canters towards us with a rifle. We pull our ponies into a walk as he draws up alongside and we stop at the lip of a wide river. When he examines our packhorse and points to a sack Morten replies, then dismounts and digs out the last can of sardines. He opens it with a knife and hands it to the guard.

"He wanted to know where we've been and was keen to scrummage around in our belongings," Morten says. "I've diverted him with the sardines." The guard smiles like a child and babbles something. "He says he's never tasted seafood before."

We ride to Tsaggan Nuur with feelings of excitement. In civilisation terms it's the end of the world, but to us the collection of wooden huts coming into view is a metropolis. The Tasman blue lake on the far side is so still, it's as if you could pull it and it would fall away like a tablecloth.

– Chapter 5 –

An encounter with a shaman

We come to a halt outside our hut in Tsaggan Nuur and our two escorts disappear into town. Mixer is pleased to see us, and we dine on fish and vodka. One of the community's loos is situated a healthy stroll from the nearest hut. It's a wooden roof with two holes in the ground, where the mound of human refuse looks like a very large stalagmite. My giardia adds a splattering of colour to it all and I amble back to Morten and Mixer, clutching the mandatory roll of loo paper.

The following morning our escorts come to bid us farewell as they're returning to the taiga. One of them has collected a black eye during the night after a fight with three of the locals. It has closed up his left eye in a marinade of blues, purples and reds, but he seems happy enough as they trot into the horizon. The Khalkha represent 80 per cent of Mongolians, but Khovsgol is occupied by Darkhat Mongolians, a minority who honour shamans, the healers whose ancient doctrine predates the Bronze Age class society. Shamanism is still practised in parts of Mongolia and Siberia.

Shamans are believed to have the power not only to cure the sick, but also to communicate with the world beyond the one we live in. They do this at ceremonies where they wear a gown, headdress and footwear that gives them the guise of a particular animal. They work with a single membrane drum and it's the sound of this that draws the spirit, which then enters the shaman, or the drum. The shaman attains an ecstatic state and demonstrates unusual physical prowess, before convulsing and falling into a form of unconsciousness where he or she is able to communicate with the spirits. After accepting the spirit the shaman becomes its mouthpiece and medium.

It's the summer solstice and we've been invited to a shaman ceremony. We drive across the barren steppe which looks as though it's covered with a cedar-green skin. Gers weave smoke from their roofs. Gone are the winter browns and yellows. Summer has arrived and in the warm sunshine horses form circles, like open fans. They thrash the air with their heads and swipe their tails, as foals frolic between their legs. A black stallion selects a pale, chestnut mare and they both withdraw from the circle. His anatomy ripples and glistens in the sunlight as he climbs onto her back. The mares whinny, but remain in the circle standing head to head. The stallion closes his eyes. His body relaxes and is still for a moment, before he dismounts and they re-enter the circle next to each other, greeted by the other mares with audible excitement.

These horse circles appear to be unique to Mongolia. In other wildernesses, mating rituals are different. While the herd grazes, the stallion, after determining if a mare is in season, will lick the top of her legs and flanks. They stand nose to nose, squealing, and he paddles the air with his front legs. He then moves to the back of the mare and sometimes makes a couple of dummy jumps before mounting.

We judder to a stop outside a small wooden hut and get out of the Jeep. The shaman is a hunched and gnarled octogenarian-looking woman. Her back is rounded, her hands are bunched like ginger roots and the skin around her eyes is puckered. She potters about the stove, washing her hands in milk and presenting lengths of blue cloth to the wall, as if there are people there. The black stove sizzles and spits glowing sparks, flickering the wooden walls with streaks of bronze and copper light. Spirits appear to loll on the wall, throw their heads back as if gargling and vanish into the darkness.

There's an odour of must and shaved wood. The room is clean, tidy and prepared. Children climb onto a bunk bed, shuffle up next to each other and pull their heads into the collars of their deels like turtles. Their eyes hook onto the shaman's every gesture, as if she might turn into a dragon. There's no fear in their curiosity, only wonder and awe. I sit on a saddle and watch an audience of all ages settle on the floor, or lean against the wall until the room is packed, as if this is the month's main event. A final person scuttles into a cramped corner and the shaman's two apprentices clear a circle around her. They hold a robe of dripping metal into which she eases herself and a mask, crafted with meandering plumes, is carefully lowered over her face.

The spell is cast. She leaps into the air, stamps her feet and thumps her tambourine drum. The audience heaves, mesmerised and silent. The children gasp and retreat deeper into their collars as the shaman cackles, hisses and rattles her drum. She jumps and twists, and the feathers from her mask seem to become alive, as she does her rasping chant.

Two hours later three drunk Mongolians stumble through the door and stare at the shaman, their chins slumped into the necks of their deels, as if watching a video. A woman from the audience is summoned by the shaman. She crouches nervously on the floor and the shaman whips her with part of the costume. I have no idea what's going on: Morten is on the other side of the room, and I'm cut off. Hoping not to displease the shaman or her spirits, I creep outside.

Burying my chin into my deel and tugging my hands into its sleeves, I lie on the steppe and gaze at the sky, watching shooting stars. The muffled thump, thump, thump, continues but I don't want to be summoned by the shaman. My dreams are as vivid as my waking hours.

Sometimes I wake up within my dreams and need to determine if I'm awake, or asleep. I float on the ceiling or, walking across a room, look back and see myself sleeping. Some shamans use hallucinogenics. I've shied away from drugs mostly because it's not you choosing the drug, but the drug choosing you, and that's when things start to fall apart. I've smoked grass occasionally, even eaten it, but never regularly, and that's as far as I've gone except once, just before I left for Mongolia. I went to see a friend and we picked some magic mushrooms from a field by the sea. I consumed a dozen of them.

It was an extraordinary experience. A dark, oblong doorway appeared above me and I leapt through it, leaving my physical body behind. It was as if I had let go of everything I had come to know. I entered a dimension devoid of fear, permeated with serenity and full of a peaceful, omnipresent roar. It was as if I were a molecule flying through space. After a time, I found myself in the presence of a fluorescent white light. I was wholly alert and in possession of all my senses. It felt natural and I wasn't afraid. I knew I was able to communicate with this light and could ask anything, but didn't need to; I felt as If I'd come home. "I just don't want to go back," I said.

It was the only time I heard a voice. "You can stay here for as long as you want," the light replied. I don't know how long I was away, but it was as if I was taken on a journey through the galaxies and had an overwhelming sense that the unknown is natural, and that life is conscious. For some reason I eventually decided to return to my body.

I walk back into the hut to find the shaman exorcising a boy who's hunkered on the floor in front of her. The shaman lifts her arms, points at me and thumps her drum with increasing agitation. Anxious arms pull my deel and worried faces motion me to move. I am apparently in the flight path of an exorcised evil spirit: they come in through the roof and leave through the door. I shallow dive into some Mongolians who aren't impressed with my pantomime.

At the first splinters of dawn light, the shaman drops the drum and her hands perform a swaying ballet. The audience, about to leave, are so taken by this abrupt transformation that they stand like statues, watching her every movement. As her mask and costume are removed she becomes an elderly woman once again. She shuffles around the stove asking about her activities over the past six hours, apparently feeling refreshed and rejuvenated, when younger physically fit people might feel exhausted.

The next morning we start the journey back to UB and I drop Morten off with his family in Ulaan-Uul. I find a chocolate bar, rip off its packaging and slowly relish every mouthful. Our trail south is alive with a nomadic nation travelling to their summer camps, caravans of camels, yaks and cattle carrying dismantled gers and possessions. Alongside, livestock are herded by mounted family members. Horses with fat bellies graze in fetlock deep grass and it smells of summer.

I arrive back in UB three days later and have a bath. Grubby sores and colourful bruises appear, as dirt, hairs and grime are washed away. In places my curly, brown locks are knotted into clumps. I have to change the water twice before it remains transparent with me lying in it, apart from the presence of a few rogue tendrils. I must confess to being a bit of a hypochondriac. I can give myself pains worrying about my pains, and it's a while before I'm convinced that these scrubby little sores aren't the precursor to the bubonic plague.

The plague still exists in Mongolia, with cases reported in the wilderness every year, as herdsmen trot into local sum (provincial) centres feeling groggy and covered with black swelling marks. I pour some powder into the bath, leave my clothes to soak and sleep for twelve hours. I walk into Millie's, order a hamburger and see Pië sitting in the corner. Her mouth drops. "What have they done to you?" she exclaims. "You're emaciated."

"Giardia."

"You're so brown!"

"What's been going on in the world? Has NATO bombed any more embassies?"

Pië brings me up to date, but her snippets trail into a vocal blur, as a hamburger and a milkshake are placed in front of me. I look at the colours, imagine the flavours and textures, then guzzle them both.

– Chapter 6 –

A street child's warrior

A couple of days later I walk into the Café de France, which is situated between UB's centre and the ger district. It's a quiet restaurant that brings a whiff of Corsican comfort and elegance to the eastern wilderness. As I juggle the tables in my mind to find a suitable hideaway, I'm distracted by a woman waving at me; her face explodes into a smile when our eyes meet. There are three people around the table with her, one of whom is dressed as a nun.

"Have we met?" I enquire, rather tentatively.

"Christina Noble. I'm sure I know you from somewhere. Vietnam perhaps?"

"I haven't been to Vietnam."

"Well it doesn't matter," she replies, in an Irish drawl. "What are you doing here?"

"I'm here for a year seeing Mongolia."

"A year," she repeats, then announces vigorously, "I help street children."

"I've heard about your work."

"I'd like to show you our set-up," she says. "Maybe next week sometime. Give me a call." She pens her number on the back of a table napkin. "Have you read my book?"

"No," I reply.

"I'll give you a copy."

A week later I find myself pressing the buzzer to her second-floor apartment, situated in a courtyard off UB's main drag. I look up and see Christina's head and shoulders set in the centre of a large, white window frame. "Romeo," she calls out in her strong Dublin accent, "come up." I climb the concrete stairs and find her waiting in the door-way. "Ahh," she says, "if only I were twenty years younger." I smile and walk past the kitchen into a small sitting room. The floor is covered with an ivory carpet and the room is furnished with two wooden tables, some chairs and a book-shelf that contains more papers than books. "Did you read my book?" she asks, sitting cross-legged on a blue sofa, her blonde hair curling around the top of her neck.

"Incredible" I say, sitting down. Christina's early child-hood was spent in the Dublin slums; her father was an alcoholic and her mother died when she was a girl. She and her siblings were split up and sent to different institutions. Physically abused by nuns, she escaped and grew up on the streets of Dublin. She was gang raped, left for England and married, only to discover that her husband was abusive and adulterous. Three children later she left him and, after having recurring dreams about Vietnam, went there with limited funds. She founded the CNCF (Christina Noble Children's Foundation) which has rescued 80,000 children from Vietnamese streets. She has set up a similar outfit in UB.

"And that's only half of what happened. I see it all as train-ing for what I do now. What are your thoughts on religion?"

"The Jesuits put me off religion for life."

At the age of eight I was sent to a Jesuit boarding school for five years. It was an establishment governed by a long whalebone wrapped in black leather, a clever instrument that left no marks on the human body and was adminis-tered in doses of up to twelve. We called them 'cracks'.

The only time I ever saw the head priest excited or stirred, apart from when he was hitting me, was when the Pope got shot. He charged into the classroom and pro-claimed that prayers would be held in chapel after prep. As a child, and if you don't know otherwise, you think beat-ings are normal, but living with the hanging threat that you might be next can do something to you. There was evidence of the beatings every week, often every day. Boys sometimes escaped, but were returned by the police and I heard that some of these brave children were beaten for their efforts.

"The Jesuits and the nuns of St Joseph's," Christina scowls. "I was sent as a child to an institution run by nuns." Her pupils narrow into torpedoes. "I escaped from the place, but broke my leg in the process. Did you read that?"

"I thought that was fucking cool." I am drawn by her Irish charm and honesty.

"Really?" Her blue eyes light up and the adult's shield is discarded as she becomes the child inside.

"Yes." I grin, and for a moment I, too, am a child again.

"I grew up on the streets of Dublin," Christina says, "but I grew up free." As she puts a Marlboro Light in her mouth there's a knock on the door. "That'll be Bobo with the car." I climb into the back seat with Christina. Bobo, a gentle Mongolian doctor who speaks English and is dedicated to the CNCF, gets into the front. As we drive down UB's main drag fire pumps black smoke from the top of a high-rise administration building into a blue sky. On a side-road, wrinkled smoke spirals up from an open sewer hole. Two small children stop and disappear into a vent next to it. Christina glances at me. "Children live in the sewers," she says, and turns back to Bobo, who's bringing her up to date with the CNCF hospital. A woman sits on the pavement squeezing milk from her breast onto a teaspoon and forcing it down her baby's throat.

We pull into a courtyard at the other end of the city, and I follow Christina and Bobo into the small hospital. A Mongolian nurse approaches Bobo and utters something in the calm, unflappable tones of the Mongolian language. We stop at the foot of a bed where a shrunken man with a gaunt face and knitted silver-black hair is lying on his side. "He lives down in the sewers," Bobo says. "He keeps warm by sleeping against the heating pipes down there. His back has been badly burnt." The patient flinches, tries to twist his body into another position and falls back. His black eyes are like those of a dog on a veterinary table.

In a room set aside from the main wards we collect around a girl of seven or eight. Her black hair is cropped about the neck and she seems to be wearing her smartest daily outfit. Her mother sits quietly beside her, dressed in an elegant maroon deel. A nurse kneels down and slowly unravels the thick, white bandage around the girl's knee. The child is silently brave, taking her courage from her mother and us. Bobo crouches down. The area beneath the knee is putrefying, a palette of purple, blue and chocolate mint. The skin looks as if it's been gouged with a scooper.

"It doesn't look good," Christina says, and buckles her lips. The silence is difficult to disguise. The girl gasps and her face shudders into dry tears. "We're going to the ger camp. There's trouble there with one of our neighbours."

"Serious?" I ask.

"They're claiming they own a part of our camp. It's a threat to the children." We leave Bobo, and drive off to the CNCF ger camp which is situated outside the city, where the potholed road becomes a dirt track, and the track becomes the steppe. "Earlier this year, I heard that children were being abused in an orphans' institution," Christina says. "I called Eagle TV and they supplied a camera crew. I coaxed the guard into letting us in." Her jaw clenches. "We found children locked up, half naked and with scars on their bodies. We released them, got it on film and Eagle TV broadcast it. We told the world."

From a distance the ger camp looks like a small wooden fort. A burly Mongolian wearing a flat cap, black leather jacket, jeans and brown boots opens the tall gates into the barricaded compound. His face is expressionless, as if you could hit him with a baseball bat and he wouldn't flicker. "Security for the kids," Christina says. "You need someone like him out here."

We park in the inner compound and the gates are pulled shut behind us. Another barricaded door is opened and children seem to fall out from behind it, running towards Christina shouting, "Mama Tina, Mama Tina." Her large, Womble-like frame seems to embrace them all and no child is left without a hug, a touch or a nuzzle. There are six gers in the inner compound, each run by a 'ger mother'. A larger ger, the size of a small marquee, acts as the school and we attend part of a lesson before Christina bursts into guttural song. A child comes up to me, motioning with his arms to swing him around, and a short queue quickly forms behind him.

"Be careful," Christina says, "of their tiny arms, but never refuse a child's hand." The guard taps her on the shoulder and points. "It's time to deal with this problem." She rolls up her sleeves and a translator joins us. I follow them out of the compound. Christina paces ahead, her arms swinging, fists clenched.

"Do I look all right?" I ask.

"Remove the jersey from around your waist," she snaps. The four of us stop opposite a wooden hut where six Mongolians, two woman and four men, have gathered. A stocky man with impenetrable black eyes bends down and picks up an axe. He stands beside a middle-aged woman, presumably the matriarch of the group. The guard and I stand slightly back from Christina and her translator. There is a feeling of stand-off.

"I'm Christina Noble," she shouts. "You know who I am, and what I can do. Come anywhere near my children and I'll call Eagle TV." The Irish accent is formidable when employed in anger. Her words are translated. "That is our land," she says pointing to the compound. "You touch it and I'll get the police and army here. Is that fucking clear?" Her words are translated. The Mongolian matriarch looks ill at ease and the man shuffles his grip around the axe. "Try anything and I'll let Mongolia and the international community know what you've done. Have you got that in your heads?"

Christina walks over to the matriarch, fixes her with a stare and walks towards the ger camp. The three of us follow in her wake. When we arrive back at the camp Christina's anger visibly diffuses as children run up and hug her waist. A couple more feel for my hands and I can't help but smile. Christina points to a disorientated puppy standing in a barren patch of land. "I found Inkh on the main street, about to be run over. He doesn't look well, does he? Should we take him with us?"

She picks up the dog and we get into the car. "Now tell me, what are you really doing in Mongolia?"

"I woke up one morning with Mongolia in my head, as if something had placed it in my mind. At the time it seemed to be the only thing that made any sense."

"That's how *I* came to be in Mongolia. I woke up with the word and had to ask someone if Mongolia existed. Vietnam was different. I had this recurring dream." Christina and I go back to her apartment and talk about the strange reality of our dreams. "I think you've been sent to Mongolia," she says. "Where do you live?"

"Scotland, but I've been on the move, one way or another, all my life."

"You're like me then, a Gypsy. Raising funds this year is difficult. The war in Kosovo is getting a lot of publicity, but I'll raise the money even if I have to sing in every pub in Ireland." She smiles. "I'm going back to Vietnam the day after tomorrow. Will you look after my puppy?"

I get up, give Christina a hug and leave with a sick puppy.

Outside the state department store a child of maybe eight, with black, straggly hair, sits on the ground, his dark eyes appealing for generosity. Apart from a pair of shabby, tattered trousers, he is naked. I catch his eye and he follows me through the main entrance where I stop in front of the bakery counter. I put a bag of bread rolls into his dirty, black hands and he runs off, his head bobbing between the counters like flotsam disappearing in and out of the ocean waves. Two children scream at a charcoal puppy as it zigzags across the floor like a drunken adolescent.

Inkh doesn't move from the sofa for three days. He lies there, not eating or drinking, not giving even a whimper. From time to time, an eye follows me around the room and I wonder how best to tell Christina that her puppy has died. But he recovers through a therapy of sleep and antibiotics, and slowly regains his appetite. He trots behind me on my walks in the steppe outside the city and it isn't long before I return him to the ger camp.

– Chapter 7 –

The vanished holy people

The Altai Mountains in western Mongolia are home to the endangered snow leopard and Asia's largest Neolithic rock art site. Since 4000 BC the region has been important to the nomadic peoples, who used it as a pathway between Siberia and Mongolia. It served as a retreat from the winter blizzards and winds that occasionally made life on the steppe unbearable, and was a place where people found refuge after tribal battles. The valleys have been used as a burial ground down the ages, but since the demise of the nomadic empires the Altai has returned to obscurity. Now, among its naked valleys, fragments of vanished peoples can be found and, in the wind, whispers of their ways.

When I first arrived in UB, I tried to contact Atai who's director of the Tavan Bogd National Park. Maybe it was because my first two faxes were addressed to, 'Dear Altai' that I didn't receive a reply.

Before our departure for Khovsgol, Morten introduced me to Jenya, a wiry, talkative fellow in his early twenties with a knowing grin and cheeky black eyes. Half Russian, half Mongolian, he belongs to a breed exiled to social purgatory. Jenya despises missionaries, is incapable of aggression, favours apathy and has a knack of sorting out problems, as well as getting into them. I need a translator and he not only speaks English but is reliably upbeat. I buy two tickets on the airline that has an annual track record of fatal plane crashes. Jenya agrees to organise a taxi and meet me outside my hotel at 6.30 the following morning.

I collapse at 4 am after an evening of wine. What seems a moment later, my alarm goes off at 6 am and I groan as I hear the sound of torrential rain on corrugated metal. It's the rainy season. My eyes are bloodshot, my eyelids dark, glaring hammocks. I collect my pack and stumble downstairs where the receptionist who smiled at me two hours earlier tries to disguise a chuckle with her right hand.

Jenya is waiting in the front of a car and I climb into the back. Only a few steps from the hotel door the rain is so heavy that it pours off my hair onto the seat as if I've just turned off the shower. The driver murmurs something as he steers through the waterfall of rain, trying to avoid potholes in a road that resembles a stream in spate.

"He says that if there's no lightning they will fly. If there is, they will not," Jenya says, visibly disturbed. At the airport I look up at the flight departure board: nearly all flights have been cancelled except ours and one other. We shuttle to the plane as water bounces off the runway. "It should be fine." Jenya's dark eyes sweep across my face. "They've already crashed this year."

"It's four hours by plane, or five days by jeep," I mumble, climbing into the propellered aircraft. I place a cooking pot in the open ledge above the seat and sit down. The plane trundles along the runway, slowly lifts into the air and quickly reaches its cruising altitude still surrounded by impermeable fog. In one of the highest countries in the world I fall asleep, as I sometimes do when I'm afraid.

Bayan-Olgiy is an Altai province in Mongolia's western extremities, an area inhabited by Kazakhs. It is bordered by Russia in the north and China to the west and south. Our plane touches down and we disembark into a temperature 15°C hotter than UB. The Kazakhs have emerald, jade and cobalt irises. They are leaner than the Mongolians and their

The Steppe

Ovoo ceremony in Khovsgol

Otrs with an obliging reindeer
(Copyright Alan Wheeler)

Dismantling camp

Opposite page: The Dukha's home in the taiga

Saddling up

On the move

Snaking our way through the taiga

The Altai (Jenya is seated centre)

Naadam

Ger life in the Altai

The gathering at Naadam

Neolithic rock art

A petroglyph

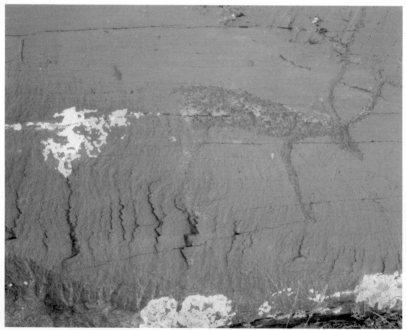

Still spinning silk in the Taklamakan

The author with the remains of a sauropod in the Gobi

skin is lighter, a shade of glazed amber. Although they wear deels, they favour brightly coloured brocaded skull caps. They are sympathetic to cats which, for a reason I haven't been able to discover, the Mongolians hate.

The sum of Olgiy nestles on the banks of a worming river, surrounded by Sicilian shaped mountains in a plateau of dust. It is hot and dry. There is no traffic in the centre but, like a magic show, a camouflage-green Jeep slams into a twin-seater motorbike and catapults its occupants into the air. Jenya and I walk into a communist building and find Atai, sporting a blue baseball cap, sitting behind a desk in a cramped office. A proud Kazakh in his forties, he has a well-trimmed moustache, a roundish face and a corpulent waistline that advertises his social position in the region. "The rock art site," Atai says, in broken but softly delivered English, "is on Russian border. Scientists sometimes come." He takes out a map. "I organise guide in two weeks. How long you here?"

"Three weeks."

"Naadam in four days," he says, folding the map and replacing it on top of a wooden cabinet. "Seven hours Jeep."

"Naadam," Jenya interjects. "Mongolian festival. Archery, wrestling and riding competitions."

"We'll go there in the meantime." As we walk outside a Muslim chant drifts across a tangerine sky, like floating silk.

Two days later we drive past diving marmots and the standing stones of ancient Mongoloid warriors, towards rippling snow-capped mountains. In his prison cell in Venice 700 years ago, Marco Polo suggested that the great Khans were secretly buried in the Altai Mountains. The whereabouts of Chinngis Khan's grave remains a mystery. When he died his body was placed in a ger and escorted by thousands of troops to an unidentified burial place. It is recorded that anybody whose path the funeral procession crossed was slaughtered to ensure secrecy. After the emperor was interred hundreds of horses were stampeded across the site

to obliterate evidence of its location. Some believe that he's buried in the Altai Mountains; others favour the idea that he lies in his home province in central Mongolia.

I turn a sleeve of rolling paper into a cigarette. We stop at an ovoo and a man with a facial skin disorder stares at me. Long black and white prickly hairs protrude through blistered, purple skin as if he's half wolf, or bear. We meet with a grin, but it seems that I am the more outlandish.

"When that policeman drove off with our passports into the mountains," says Jenya, "I thought we wouldn't see them again. Hey," he continues as our Jeep moves off, "there's petrol leaking from that jerry can." He points to the floor in front of us and circles the leak with a finger. "Nothing we can do," he decides and lights up a cigarette. Dust swirls around the Jeep. My forehead is freckled with droplets of perspiration. My shirt clings to my skin and sweat trickles down my neck.

"You know, the Mongolians in UB ask about you, what you're doing here," Jenya says, as we pass some camels.

"There's this children's story," he continues, "about why the camel is always looking around, as if waiting for someone to return." He unscrews the cap of his water bottle. "The camel once had antlers and was beautiful. One day a deer asked the camel if he could borrow his antlers for a party. The camel agreed as long as they were returned in the morning, but the deer never returned and that is why the camel is always looking, to see if you've come to return his antlers."

When we reach our ger I watch podgy raindrops land on the stove and puff into tiny balls of steam. Kazakh gers are almost twice the size of the Mongolians' and their roofs are higher. The roof support poles are curved at the point where they join the circular framework and bright wall hangings cover the walls. Coloured rugs decorate the ground, a hunting eagle sits on a perch and the lady of the ger is, like her Mongolian counterparts, attentive to her family and visitors.

The Kazakhs wash before and after they've eaten, albeit with a communal rag. They live a more comfortable nomadic life than the Mongolians and, rather than noodle soup prefer horse leg (which is strangely sweet), floppy liver, rubbery, spiralling intestines and soggy pasta. I sit by the lake under a vibrant night sky, undress and walk into the cool water. While I'm floating on my back, as if gravity doesn't exist, and staring at the stars, two children appear out of the darkness and I return to the shore. I dress and they escort me back to the gers, singing on either side of me. The Milky Way cummerbunds across the night sky, as comets firework and satellites crawl. The moon and stars are inverted in the lake.

A small, round, bright light emerges from the mountains. "What's that?" I ask.

"A Jeep," an adolescent replies, but the ball of light leaves the summits, moves into space and sails slowly from west to east. I become aware that the occupants of the three gers are gathered around me, transfixed by this mysterious object which has a short flaring tail. As the ball of light reaches the peak of its trajectory, the night sky transforms into day, as five vast channels of light bridge the sky's horizons. No one says a word as the ball moves slowly out of our field of vision. Night gradually reclaims its character as the stars and their constellations reappear. The sky glitters and the herders return inside.

Jenya walks over with a bowl of milk tea. "In 1997," he says, "I accompanied a Danish photographer to the Dukha's winter camp. We saw a large, circular object surrounded by a grey light hovering above a mountain a kilometre away. It was there for about thirty seconds before it flew off. No sound. No flashing lights. Neither the reindeer herders, the Dane nor I had seen anything like it." He lights a cigarette. "The shamans got very excited."

I put my sleeping bag on the ger's floor, roll over and gaze at the stars through the round hole in the roof. A bee-

tle walks over the bridge of my hand, stops as if in reflection, then scurries away.

The Russian-born painter, Nicholas Roerich, travelled 15,500 miles through Inner Asia between 1923 and 1928. While he was in Mongolia, on 5 August 1926, he wrote this in his travel journal:

> *Something remarkable! In the morning about half past nine some of our caravaners noticed a big black eagle flying above us. At the same moment another of our caravaners remarked, 'There is something far above the bird' ... We all saw, in a direction from north to south, something big and shiny reflecting the sun, like a huge oval moving at great speed. Crossing our camp this thing changed in its direction from south to west ... We even had time to take out our field glasses and saw quite distinctly an oval form with shiny surface.*

Roerich completed 500 works on that trip. His paintings are lonely, intimate and spectacularly psychedelic, as if each canvas represents a fragment of his spiritual quest. In his book, *Shambhala*, he recounts stories told by the region's indigenous peoples about the Agharti, or the 'vanished holy people', a race who went to live underground and discovered a network of tunnels, allegedly leading to the subterranean kingdom of Shambhala, or Shangri-La.

Another in the region fleeing from Bolsheviks was Ferdinand Ossendowski, a Polish scientist. In his *Beasts, Men and Gods*, published in 1922, he tells of a Prince Chultun Beyli describing how, 60,000 years ago, a holy man had led a tribe of his followers deep into the earth, and how, through his wisdom, power and the labour of his people, Agharta had flourished as a paradise. Roerich and Ossendowski never met.

During his travels in the Altai, Roerich was led to a large tomb encircled by stones (a characteristic of most Altai tombs). His guide explained that this used to be an entrance to the tunnels, but although the Agharti had sealed it behind them, the sound of muffled bells and singing could

sometimes be heard from what were purportedly their underground temples. Roerich was told that through these passages the Agharti could travel to distant countries on missions of goodwill.

Was it perhaps more than coincidental that in 1935, shortly before the Second World War, the Roerich Peace Pact was established, which obligated nations to respect museums, cathedrals, universities and libraries, in the same way as hospitals? Did Roerich, mystic, painter, writer, traveller and a member of the Theosophical Society, make contact with the mythical Agharti?

Roerich goes on to record similar tales of these subterranean dwellers in China's Turpan and Khotan regions, and mentions a Mongolian buryat lama who was accompanied through a narrow secret passage to Shambhala. Roerich enquired if anyone could see the Agharti, and was informed that they could, but only if a person's thoughts were as pure and courageous as theirs.

At one point Roerich met a lama and questioned him. Roerich understood the concept of a heavenly Shambhala but what about the earthly Shambhala based on these subterranean tales? Did these tunnels lead to Shambhala and, if not, why hadn't Shambhala been discovered in a world where all physical geography had been explored? The lama replied that Shambhala was a heavenly domain far beyond the ocean, a particularly ambiguous, but guarded response, and went on to explain that many people searched for Shambhala but only those whose karma was ready could succeed. In another source, Shamballa (spelt differently), is referred to in ancient books as the White Island, and is located in the Gobi, where it exists in etheric matter.

I avoid a breakfast of goat's guts, pony's brains and floating human hair with a bold slanting smile. Nomads ride past stone burial mounds that look like giant molehills, and it's almost as if you can see unicorns frolicking in the silvery

mist around them. We set off and a flickering lake appears in the distance, with what appears to be a flock of scattered flamingoes along the shore, but is in fact a town of felt of 500 gers at their summer camp. We could be anywhere between 3000 BC and today.

Our driver clasps the steering wheel as we lurch across a river. I watch him glance at the Russian truck which has stalled to our right and his eyes expand as water flows over our Jeep's bonnet. Water seeps under the doors and I lift my legs off the floor as the vehicle starts to stall. The driver's feet slam the pedals while his left hand wrestles with the gearstick and his right hand works the steering wheel as if it were a combination padlock. The engine coughs, the Jeep surges forward and he slowly navigates to the other side. He throws open the door, gets out and grins with evident relief.

We join hundreds of mounted nomads attired in deels of all colours and shades, who look like the advance guard of an invasion force as they canter, trot and walk, in a straggling fog of dust and fractured images. "Naadam," Jenya says. "It's been tradition for two thousand years." The nomads are collecting behind a cluster of gers, where hundreds of horses are hobbled together. Brawny wrestlers stomp from side to side, then lunge at each other with springy propulsion. Our host, a former champion wrestler, has slaughtered fifty sheep and four horses for the day's banquet. He is being presented with a camel by one of his guests, as children bait chained, snarling wolf cubs and falcons for sale perch alongside golden eagles on stumpy posts.

I absorb the views of fanning horizons and listen to the undertones of a foreign land as a number of Kazakhs gesture their interest in my maps. A mounted adolescent wearing a brown deel and a Russian soldier's cap beckons me to climb on. He leapfrogs onto the horse's haunches and a small stone lands on my scalp. An elderly Kazakh wearing a purple, fox-lined hat taps me on the shoulder and points into

the wilderness, as if I should be looking at something. I remove my binoculars and see a ball of dust under a spine of mountains.

"Children's horse race – bareback," Jenya says.

A hundred or so horses are galloping towards us and a buzzing crowd has formed around a makeshift finishing line. A lone policeman tries in vain to keep control of the nomads as a child, who looks about ten, crosses the line almost airborne. Relations rush forward, at which point the policeman begins to beat the offending individuals with his horse whip. The crowd giggles and cheers, as the rest of the young riders charge over the line and jovial chaos ensues. I borrow an auburn horse and canter off into the wilderness.

I can't remember if this is the ger to which I've been invited. I don't recognise anyone but this Kazakh family seems happy to see me. I'm offered some kumiss, a brew of fermented mare's milk that tastes like alcoholic yoghurt. A teenager is struggling to fix a shattered perspex motorbike windshield. I gesture that I'm camped nearby and have some Superglue. He leads me outside and offers me a horse. Kazakh mounts are real horses, designed for people of my height, and I gallop to my camp, where Jenya and the driver are asleep by the lake next to a smoking fire.

I empty the contents of my survival bag onto the floor of the tent, dig out the Superglue and return to the ger. Pointing to my eyes and fingers, I explain the dangers of the glue, then we apply the liquid along the cracks and use our hands as clamps to hold the pieces together. Encouraged by this success, a man takes me outside to the mangled motor-bike and puts a spanner in my hand. I look concerned, tug a few wires and swing a bulb backwards and forwards then, with a smile and a shrug, return the spanner.

I canter back to our camp and find Jenya talking to a stern-looking border guard on a black horse with diamond flashes. "He says that you were seen close to the border," Jenya says. "You are forbidden to go up this valley, or up

into the mountains behind us." I grunt my agreement. The guard looks at me and rides off. Fourteen of our neighbours ride up and parade in front of our camp in one long line. Jenya explains that they want their photograph taken so I comply with a volley of snaps and they trot off.

We return to Olgiy where a man introduces himself as a journalist for the region's radio station. He enquires if I would be happy to comment on Naadam. Jenya and I follow him into his office, sit down on a tired, torn sofa, an old microphone is put into my hands and the journalist starts his interview while Jenya translates. I tell him my thoughts about Naadam and he asks what I'm doing in Mongolia. I explain about the reindeer herders, the rock art and my hopes to see the dinosaurs in the Gobi. When his questions draw to a close we leave and I put Jenya on a plane to UB. Atai organises a jeep and guide, but money is tight and I'm going to have to rely on my Mongolian dictionary.

We head into the mountains, past lolloping camels, and arrive in a valley denuded of life. My guide points to a mountain and we climb out of the vehicle to head off in different directions, looking for rock art. Some time later, I turn to see my guide waving his arms frantically from a far-off ridge. He runs across the mountain and stops in front of me. His face is haggard, his eyes bulge and his body heaves; he looks as if he's completed a forced march. He shakes his head at me and, while pointing to Russia, turns his arms into a rifle. He points it at me, pulls an imaginary trigger and cries, "*Bang, bang, bang.*" He grabs my elbow and hurries me off the mountain to the safety of our Jeep.

"Do you know where this rock art site is?" My guide's expression is a collage of embarrassment. "And Asia's largest site?" He clears his throat and points hopefully at the horizon.

I want to see this site and my guide means well; at least he appears to know the general direction. We drive past herds of camels, deeper into the mountains. Isolated

nomads seem to float over crescents, or hover above long needles of marsh grass which, in a breeze, look like beds of flowing porcupine quills. We stop outside the coloured doorway of a lonely ger. I watch the guide and the driver visibly recover as we are offered milk tea and bits of goat: meat is to the Mongolian peoples what wind is to sailing. One of the herders knows where the rock art site is and agrees to take us there.

In the soothing light of a low morning sun, I climb up a hill scented with pockets of thyme and look down at engravings of reindeer and elk, the beginnings of a vast gallery of ancient graffiti, like a huge photograph album. Most rocks contain just one drawing of an animal – an ibex, a horse, sometimes a deer – coloured with splashes of yellow, green, orange and red lichen.

I walk as if I've dropped something precious on the ground, studying chiselled drawings of mammoths, rhinoceroses, archers, dodos, circular symmetry, battle scenes, hunting horsemen and spotted creatures, all portrayed with the simplicity of a small child's artwork. One rock face might contain a dozen such etchings and I sit down on a rock that was once a canvas. In a barren wilderness devoid of any trees or shrubbery it's hard to imagine this was once lush, but long ago this region was covered with forests, juniper bushes, ground shrubs and plants, all of them providing a habitat for a variety of wild animals and a hunting ground for Neolithic man. The rocky gullies burst into life and I am in the company of bygone peoples, from a lost age.

I remove a few leaves of paper, a sepia pastel and take tracings of some of the smaller petroglyphs. A few hours later we drive off and turn into a valley freckled with gers, like golf balls randomly displayed on a putting green. "My family here somewhere," my guide says. He smiles, flicks through the pages of the dictionary and his finger trawls down a page. "You, guest, yes?" We stop outside a ger.

I bend into the entrance and emerge into a circle of stares. My guide indicates that I sit next to the ageing family potentate. I'm offered a bowl of milk tea and a grey goat is hustled through the doorway, held in the grip of a wiry middle-aged man. The patriarch mumbles a Muslim prayer and as he finishes the seated family members open the palms of their hands and finish with a downward washing motion over their faces. Meanwhile, the well-behaved goat slowly grinds its jaw.

"Photograph?"

"No," I reply, as the goat is led outside. Its legs are bound and its head pointed towards the setting sun. As the head is supported over a large cooking vessel, the neck is pulled back and the executioner grips its mouth with his left hand. The knife glints in a fiery, orange sun before slicing through the artery and blood hoses into the bowl.

"In your honour."

I catch my distorted reflection in the swirling blood. Snorting grunts heave through the goat's nostrils, its hind legs kick frenetically and I watch the life drain from its eyes. The neck is tilted and the last trickles of blood drop into the bowl. The executioner taps the hind legs and decapitates the animal, laughing with a woman who's breast-feeding her baby. Children mock my facial expression, kidnap the head and run behind a ger.

The goat is skinned and hung from the roof where it falls into the hands of a skilled surgeon. A stunningly beautiful woman in her early twenties with oasis-blue eyes and long, silky black hair walks over to the corpse and holds a bowl in front of the goat's belly. She removes two light grey sacs which fall into the bowl. She runs a blade through them to reveal a package of purple, blue and grey shapes. She and another woman carefully dissect the intestines, as if each organ has a special role for their survival. A buzzard fledgling picks at a dead squirrel and the children, in French Revolutionary style, have mounted the goat's head on a pike

and are burning the hair in the long yellow flames of a fire. All that remains of the dismantled carcass are the hind legs and spine which sway from the roof as people walk past.

Two eating circles are formed inside a ger, one made up of women, the other of men. Both circles sit around a large communal bowl filled with goat swimming in its own sauce. "Male," my guide says, pointing to the brain, liver and intestines in our bowl, "privilege."

"Good," I reply.

"Women eat meat," he continues, with a grin.

I think this is a clever female conspiracy, as my fingers hover above something that twists, glide past the cerebellum and select a piece of the liver. There are flurries of laughter as the goat is gobbled and marrow is carefully extracted from snapped bones. If Mongolians sound as if they have spittle between their tongue and lips, then the Kazakhs cluck.

I'm told that it's only the second time they can remember a foreigner in the area. I lie on the floor and fall asleep. The dark-haired, blue-eyed angel gets up in the obscurity of the night and goes to the aid of her grandfather. Before climbing back into bed she removes her gown, which falls to the floor, steps over me and slips under her blanket.

After a morning of vodka toasts we drive back to Olgiy. A man in his fifties with iridescent jade eyes asks what I'm doing here and I explain. "I know you," he retorts. "You were on the radio."

Fifteen minutes after my plane to UB has taken off, two sweaty Mongolians walk down the aisle looking for a seat, as if they've been hiding in the loo. I remember Alan Wheeler telling me that he was on a flight when two Mongolians whispered derogatory remarks into the ears of a Kazakh. The Kazakh smashed one of the Mongolians in the head and a fist fight began among the thirty or so passengers. The plane landed to refuel and the pilots lost their

tempers. The passengers looked contrite and promised to behave, but when they took off again the Kazakh snarled an insult at the Mongolians and another brawl started above Mongolia.

At our refuelling stop in Khovsgol, two blonde French women decide that they've arrived in UB. They point to their cases while a hostess explains that UB is still a further two hours away. Apparently satisfied, they put on their shades and sunbathe on the runway. Horses are parked around the airport and people sell airag through the fence. The passengers board the plane, except for the French women who are lying in the sun. A hostess climbs out of the plane and asks if they'd still like to come. We land at UB and a Mongolian man, not content with his place at the back of the queue, pushes his way to the exit at the front.

I hail a cab into UB and in a small hotel find a grotty room with a soiled mattress. I drop my pack on the floor and get into the shower. The water is tepid, but I feel as though I'm in five-star accommodation: for the first time in weeks, I can wash. The luxury of having a private loo to cater for my giardia brings a smile to my face.

I ring Hans and Pië. "You're invited to dinner," they tell me. "We placed your invitation with various people in case they spotted you."

There's something exhilarating about walking off a plane after a month in the wilderness, your whereabouts unknown and the time of your return unplanned, and finding you're invited to a dinner party in an hour's time. Hans and Pië rent an apartment that has the feeling of western city design with calm, inverted side-lighting. Pië takes my arm and leads me to a table of gravelax, champagne and pâté. Friendly expats say a warm hello and I feel that I can let my sixth sense go off duty for the evening.

"Hey man," Morten says.

"You're not supposed to be back for months," I reply.

"I know," he says between gritted teeth, perching on the

side of a blue sofa, "but a Mongolian came after me with a Kalashnikov. This Mongolian woman began singing a love song to me in front of a group of people. I was told that the husband was drunk, last seen cursing my name and loading his Kalashnikov. I fled into the night and found a ger in another valley where the family looked after me. They said this man was after my blood." Morten is noticeably on edge. "And two drunk Mongolians gave me a hard time on the bus, so I punched one of them in the face. I was so pissed off by then and anyway, it shut them up." Morten leans back into the sofa. "Jenya said you saw this night-time phenomenon in the Altai."

"The whole sky lit up — must have been either a rocket launch from Kazakhstan, or a UFO. My giardia's back."

"There are two pills to cure that, but if you drink alcohol within forty-eight hours of taking them, you have a feeling of immediate death," Morten says gleefully and refills his glass. I'm not sure what's worse, having a feeling of immediate death, or going without wine for two days in the only city for 1000 square miles where it's available. "When Alan got back from the reindeer herders," Morten continues, "Kim made him take his clothes off before she let him into the apartment."

"Married life," I grin.

"No, man. He was covered with lice."

Last night I was on the other side of Mongolia dining on freshly executed goat in a place where few westerners have ever set foot. Now, among the comforting chatter of the English, French and Danish languages, I fill my glass with a fine burgundy, put some pâté on a piece of toast and savour every mouthful. Time travel at its best.

From goat's brain, vodka and giardia to gravelax and champagne. The extremities of human society are working against my biology and I wake up groping for a light switch. I stumble to the loo, crouch naked over its urine-scented rim and vomit with such fury, it's as if my insides are trying

to exit through my mouth. I wake up in daylight, completely disorientated, with the sound of someone knocking at the door.

"It's Morten. Are you all right?"

"Giardia ... wine ... beer. How did you find me?" I groan, from the mattress on the floor.

"Tried the hotels. We thought you'd been beaten up by the Mongolians on your way back last night."

"I'm fine. I mean, you know what I mean," I grunt. "I'm just going to lie here." It's an effort to utter the words. The caring attention of a small expat community in one of the remotest parts of the planet is endearing. With that thought I slip into the mattress's body mould, put my head under the pillow and shiver.

– Chapter 8 –

Bones, stones and flints

Mongolia is like a living museum. In other countries tribal cultures have been diluted, forced to capitulate to the whims of modern progress or polluted by war. Mongolia has survived, frozen, a time warp where people exist with the land and appear the happier for it. Its peoples have maintained their culture, their lifestyle and traditions for more than 2000 years, from a time when Romans ruled the known world and before the birth of Christianity, or Islam.

In cultural terms Mongolia's survival is a miracle, particularly on the geographical scale it occupies today: over 600,000 square miles or, in European terms, the size of France, Spain, Britain and Italy combined. Imagine one-sixth of the United States cordoned off, so the native American Indians could live as they did for thousands of years before the arrival of Europeans.

And then there are the dinosaurs. Mongolian nomads who happened upon dinosaur remains handed down stories of giant dragons who lived in the sky and died when they touched the earth. Michael Novacek, a palaeontologist from the American Museum of Natural history, says, "Mongolia is one of the world's great places for dinosaurs. They represent a lost world. For me, they are so fascinating because elements of our modern world emerged in the time of the dinosaurs, things common like flowering plants and birds.

They demonstrate in multidimensional terms where we come from. We are all rooted in the time of the dinosaurs."

Roy Chapman Andrews put the Gobi's dinosaurs on the map and made himself a household name in the process. He'd been inspired by suggestions that Asia was the dispersal centre for mammalian life and arrived in the Gobi with 23 cars, 150 camels and dozens of porters. He led five expeditions between 1922 and 1930 before the Chinese and the USSR slammed their doors on the west. Between 1946 and 1990 several Mongolian, Russian and Polish joint expeditions were led into the Gobi, each highly successful. When the political doors reopened in 1989 this extraordinary part of the planet was again accessible to western scientists, and in the last decade the Mongolians have teamed up with American and Japanese palaeontologists.

I really want to see these dinosaurs. My previous arrangements for the Gobi have fallen through, for one reason or another, and I want to go with scientists who know what they're looking for. The palaeontologist Barsbold, whom I met shortly after my arrival in Mongolia, suggested I contact one of his colleagues in case there might be an opportunity to accompany a team from the Institute of Palaeontology to the Gobi on a fossil-finding trip.

In between my excursions to the taiga and the Altai, I called Barsbold's colleague, who seemed happy for me to join them sometime in August, but the dates and indeed the trip itself were, in true Mongolian manner, vague and sketchy. I call her again and she tells me that the trip's going ahead in a week's time and we agree to meet at the Natural History Museum the following day to discuss it in more detail.

Because it's a Sunday, the museum is closed to the public so I wait on the steps outside the main entrance until a skinny woman arrives. She has an angular face and wears slightly tinted glasses that still reveal conker dark eyes. She doesn't smile and seems irritated as she unlocks the door,

and I feel a sense of foreboding while we wind our way along corridors bordered with glass cabinets containing dinosaur fossils, bones and eggs, and rooms exhibiting dinosaur skeletons. She removes a cluster of keys, opens a beige door in front of us and I follow her into a small office, where she sits behind a desk and I perch on the edge of a flimsy wooden chair. Somehow I know that we are not about to discuss the trip's details.

"The expedition has been cancelled," she says, with dismissive brevity.

I shut my eyes momentarily. "Why?"

"It just has."

"But I thought you said that it was all organised." She looks at me without answering. "I've tried everyone. Do you know anybody who can help?"

"There's a palaeontologist going next week." She picks up the phone and dials. No answer. "Her name is Naraa," she says, writing down a number and handing it to me. "Try her."

I mumble my thanks, but feel like shouting at her, as she closes the door behind me. I call Jenya and ask him to try the number I've been given every thirty minutes. An hour later the phone goes in my room. It's Jenya. "She'll meet you in half an hour."

Naraa picks us up at an intersection and I like her instantly. A touch on the chubby side, with podgy fingers, she has charcoal eyes that seem to glitter with resilience and enthusiasm. As Jenya explains how my plans have collapsed she shakes her head sympathetically, then turns and gives an auspicious grin, before speaking to Jenya. "She says that she's taking a German couple in two days' time and that you can come." I want to hug her.

Nara is fifty-two and one of Mongolia's top palaeontologists who has worked in the Gobi for more than 30 years. When she was selected in 1966 to study palaeontology in what was then Leningrad, no one in Mongolia knew what

palaeontology was: they thought she was going to learn history. On expeditions into the Gobi she has excavated more than 71 freshwater turtles, tarbosaurus, dinosaur eggs, and in 1994 she found 16 protoceratops hatchlings grouped together in a nest, providing clues as to how dinosaurs raised their young.

We park outside a block of flats and climb the concrete steps to her third-floor apartment where we sit down on a sofa and a lanky man walks in. "I speak English," he says, unfolding a large map across a round table. "I'm organising this trip." I get up and stand beside him, as Naraa draws a trail across the Gobi with a finger to indicate her proposed route. It's not the best time to participate in a 1860-mile excursion into the Gobi: Russia has stopped pumping petrol into Mongolia and reserves have all but been consumed, with long queues of cars waiting outside the few petrol stations.

"What about petrol?" I ask.

"We'll fill up on the way."

"If there's hardly any petrol in UB, there's not likely to be any elsewhere," I reply, not pointing out that most of the time we'll be in the desert and that I really don't think that there'll be much petrol there either. He looks befuddled, as if the current petrol crisis has somehow avoided his attention. "We need to take petrol with us," I continue, envisaging the disintegration of another Gobi trip.

He admirably recognises the munificence of his oversight. "I will find petrol," he announces gravely.

"Who else is coming apart from the German couple, Naraa and me?"

"Baba, the driver," he answers. "I'll meet you at 9 am on Monday, at the Germans' flat."

I arrive at the address given to me by Naraa at 8.45am, climb the concrete stairs to the fifth-floor apartment and knock. A man in his early forties with a round face, blond hair and a spongy beard opens the door. "Thomas Zergiebel, and my wife, Ajusch," he says, introducing me to a short,

chirpy Mongolian woman. I place my pack and a cardboard box full of grocery supplies on the floor. "We met as students at university in Budapest," he continues in fragmented, but coherent English. "We live in Germany, but are here visiting family."

"I'm really looking forward to this trip," I say as I sit down.

"My English not so good. Speak slowly."

"Sorry. Have you been dinosaur hunting before?"

"I am amateur palaeontologist. Have visited sites in Europe. Found nothing."

"Do you think we'll find anything in the Gobi?"

Thomas frowns reflectively and shakes his head slowly. "I don't know." He pauses, as if lost in his past endeavours to find dinosaur remains. "Am happy to find dinosaur tooth."

"Me too," I reply. "Over the moon."

Nine o'clock becomes ten, ten becomes eleven and eleven becomes midday – still no Naraa, driver, vehicle or organiser. Thomas and I have bonded, as we tell ourselves to be patient and that all will be well. I go for a walk and return an hour later. Still nothing. I look out of the window into the courtyard below and watch a boy goose-stepping with a nearly finished bottle of vodka in his left hand. A girl with dark, matted hair wearing a mouldy, green jersey riddled with holes sits in a pile of rubbish and plucks out an apple core. A man wrapped in torn clothes, his body contorted by the rigours of street nomadism, crouches over a dying fire warming his bandaged hands.

Two o'clock turns into three. Thomas's face is suffused with a peachy sienna and he looks as if he's about to pull the hairs of his beard out, one by one. Then there's a knock on the door and Naraa enters, grinning, wearing brown shorts, a beige shirt, walking boots and a sandy, palaeontological hat. She's followed by our organiser. "Let's go," he says, looking pleased with himself. He's six hours late and completely unperturbed. Truly, time doesn't exist in Mongolia. The scowl that Thomas and I shoot in his direc-

tion as we gather up our supplies is the epitome of com-
pressed frustration. I walk down the stairs and bump into a
small, white mini-bus that looks as if it's on the way to the
scrapheap. The organiser pulls the back door open.

"We're going in this?" I tentatively ask.

"I have been," the organiser triumphantly proclaims,
pointing to the motley collection of jerry cans, oil drums and
other containers that line the sides of the mini-bus, "to every
petrol station in the city." He's done well. I just hope there's
enough. "This is Baba," he says. A short robust man with a
broad smile, wearing a pair of dark glasses, shakes my hand.

I pay the organiser the agreed fee of US$300, which is a
very good price. One dubious fellow proposed the fee of
US$3,000 for a similar trip. We put our packs and supplies
into the bus and climb onto the back seats. Naraa gets into
the front, Baba turns the key in the ignition and heads
south out of the city, passing long queues of cars outside
petrol stations.

Naraa and Ajusch chat enthusiastically, with bullet
translations from Mongolian into German by Ajusch.
Thomas smiles and nods his head. At the city's outskirts,
two armed policeman with old rifles wave us down outside
a hut. Thomas leans over and says something to his wife, as
if asking a question.

"What's happening?" I ask, impatient to leave UB behind.

"Must report here when return," he replies.

"Why?"

"Check we haven't the plague."

And we head off into the steppe.

We drive south for two days, stopping at a few petrol
pumps to see if we can replenish some of our empty jerry
cans. Nothing. It seems that apart from a dribble of petrol in
UB, Mongolia is fuel-less. The green steppe fades into a pebbly
terrain as we travel through the north Gobi into the middle
Gobi, where any evidence of green disappears altogether and
distant, shimmering mountains, like Mediterranean archipela-
gos, herald the beginning of the desert.

Thomas explains to me that the Flaming Cliffs, which Roy Chapman Andrews discovered to be a dinosaur mine in 1922, have been raped bare by tourists. We're going into the deep south Gobi where few people, other than scientists, have ever been. He tells me that Naraa has spent many summers alone in the Gobi doing research and that she's discovered a species of turtle which bears her name. Thomas is not my translator and as Ajusch, Naraa and Baba don't speak English, communication is difficult. If I want to acquire information I ask Thomas who translates to Ajusch. She then translates from German into Mongolian to Naraa, who reflects for a moment, and the process is repeated backwards. I don't want to bother him with my questions.

Life on this planet began as single-celled organisms 3.8 billion years ago. In an attempt to replicate pre-life Dr Stanley Miller, an American scientist, carried out experiments which support the idea that the first amino acids could have been formed from ammonia, methane and hydrogen in the earth's primitive atmosphere. Miller sent sparks (lightning) through a mixture of these gases in steam and afterwards found compounds of organic matter.

Three and half billion years later plants grew on the land and backboned animals walked the earth. The first dinosaurs emerged 228 million years ago during the Triassic, a period that introduced sharks, lobsters, beetles, bony fish and evergreens, such as the pine and ginkgo. Science has recently discovered that dinosaurs were warm-blooded and probably covered in tiny feathers, like giant fluffy lizards.

Under a flaming white sun, 30 per cent more luminous than it was nearly four billion years ago, we stop in the desert and I wrap a blue sarong over my scalp. Naraa and Thomas walk off in different directions, their hands behind their backs, heads lowered towards the ground. The heat prickles my skin and dust tickles my nose. Feeling slightly sceptical, I imitate them. A while later Naraa calls me over and opens the palm of her left hand to reveal fragments of

dinosaur bones. The white matter I've collected is dismissed as rock crustaceans and discarded. With stern emphasis, Naraa stomps across the ground, shakes her head and frowns severely at me, before showing me the correct palaeontological walking posture.

The orange canyon walls look as if they've been frescoed and the ground sometimes collapses underneath me. Desert mountain outcrops seem to float like pumice into a far-reaching haze, as dust pillars perform a pirouette and run off. Naraa walks over and reveals in her hands the lower jawbone of a protocerotops, a large herbivorous dinosaur, encased in sedimentary rock. Protocerotops, or 'first-horned dinosaurs', were small, stocky creatures with a large parrot beak and a broad well-developed bony frill extending at the back of the head. I examine each tooth in turn and an unintentional "Wow" slips from my lips. Naraa grins and the string of her palaeontological hat swings under her chin. She lifts her excavating pick into the air, points it like a wizard and beckons me to follow.

The next morning we rise at 5 am and continue searching around our camp. Fragments of dinosaur eggshells litter the ground, prolific as dandelions in a meadow. Naraa walks slowly with her head bent down. She points to a rock and with her index finger explains, by indicating to my back and hands, that we are looking at the remains of an oviraptor, probably its spine and claw. Oviraptor translates as 'egg thief' – small dinosaurs some 6 feet in length with a parrot-like skull and a toothless beak. They were first discovered by Roy Chapman Andrews in 1923 and differed little from other small theropods, except for the presence of fused collar bones that resembled those of birds.

Naraa kneels down and marks out a neat circle in the sand, before digging a shallow trench. She brushes the dust away and points to her head: a dinosaur skull. A whole world is buried here. She brushes around the bone with such concentration it's as if she's exposing a landmine, but

the bone crumbles in her fingers and she shakes her head. Sixty-five million years of the Gobi's elements have taken its toll on this skull. She carefully buries her discovery and we walk back to the mini-bus.

We drive through an enormous sand dune and tack across the desert's cratered floor, as gazelles run alongside; we bounce into the flickering crucible. "On previous expedition," Thomas says, "Naraa and Russian truck stuck in sand."

"Here?" I feel parched.

"She walk 30 kilometres in twelve hours to find water."

"How is our water?"

"Naraa knows wells." Thomas mops his forehead with a damp rag.

"Where?"

"She knows."

"Petrol?" I glance over at the collection of jerry cans and diesel drums stacked on the floor around us.

"Enough, she think. Baba not sure," Thomas replies. Naraa turns around and grins audaciously. A herd of camels breaks up in front of us, startled by our presence. In a brutal terrain that is intolerant of excuses, we stop in the burning sun, build a small ovoo from dinosaur bones, drink a bottle of vodka and sing 'Happy Birthday' to Thomas.

Deserts hum, but it's not a silent hum; it's as if they're angry at something they once had and have lost. Red arrowheads, white hand chisels and beige axeheads freckle the ground. It's not difficult to imagine *homo erectus* in his prime, hunched and squatting at the base of some fern trees on the shallow rise in front of me, sculpting flint stones into weapons and tools. Perhaps this was once a masonry and a social point for these extinguished peoples. It's an incredible feeling to pick up an axe that's been lying on the floor for a million years and stroke a finger around its edges, knowing that science says, "This was made by one of our ancestors".

Homo erectus thrived on this planet for 900,000 years until they disappeared 100,000 years ago. Skull fragments

unearthed elsewhere show they had a smaller brain than *homo sapiens*, but larger than *Australopithecus*, his precursor, who existed four million years ago. *Homo sapiens* have been around for perhaps a mere 150,000 years. We're placental mammals and one of the youngest species on the planet. While our planet's natural ecosystems have declined by about 33 per cent in the last 30 years, the ecological pressure of *homo sapiens* on earth has increased by about 50 per cent and now exceeds the biosphere's regeneration rate.

In the World Wide Fund for Nature's *Living Planet Report* of 2000, the ecosystem is divided into three categories: forest, freshwater and marine. The report shows declines for the period between 1970 and 1999. Forest includes 319 species populations and shows a population fall of about 12 per cent. Freshwater has around 194, which plummeted by 50 per cent, and marine about 217, which dived by 35 per cent. Forest areas saw a reduction of almost 11 per cent. And between 1996 and 2000 the population of *homo sapiens* increased from 5.7 billion to 6 billion. These statistics are deeply disturbing. The planet's balance sheet has gaping holes in it and they can only get worse. What are these figures going to look like in fifty years, let alone a hundred? It seems appropriate to remember the words of the physiologist J. Z. Young, "The entity that remains intact, and of which we all form a part, is not the life of one of us, but in the end the whole of life upon the planet".

The Gobi looks like the bottom of an ocean. In the dusty desolation there is a field of green grass in front of us, and it's not a mirage. I cup my hand, drink spring water, splash it over my face and feel grass against my skin. The horizon consumes a neon sun in a sea of delicate pink and a perfect black semi-circle sits across its bows – an eclipse, and what a place to see it from. Right on cue, a wolf howls from behind us before the sky turns purple and is obliterated by the stars of the night.

Pink canyons rise out of the pale, orange desert and fall into a gorge that was once alive with water and life. Dinosaur bones splatter the chalky red ground, as if jettisoned from a dustbin. It's like walking around London's Natural History Museum thinking, "Mmm, I think I'll take that" and leaving with the security guards saluting you. Where an overhang has collapsed, skeletons avalanche down the sides. Huge bones are framed in the wall. A cluster of baby turtles lies abandoned, and it's as if you can hear their last gasp. Tailbones compete for my attention with the relics of previous expeditions where this, or that skull, has been removed, leaving columns of vertebrae spinning into the earth. It takes three people three days to excavate a small dinosaur and fifteen people a month to excavate a large one. Evidence of poaching is rife and Naraa doesn't know who's buying the skeletons, or how they make it out of the country, but the money leads to China and Japan.

She finds a velociraptor skull embedded in rock and Thomas sprints past me to join her, as if someone's chasing him. Velociraptor Mongoliensis, or 'fast-running robber', had a long narrow skull with jaws filled with tightly packed rows of bladed teeth. These theropods might have hunted in packs like wolves and used their sharp claws as raking weapons to tear open the stomachs of their prey. I sit cross-legged next to the enormous femur of a sauropod, and stroke the palm of my hand over the bone. Sauropods, herbivores with small heads, long narrow necks, massive bodies, huge tails and legs like tree trunks, lived on this planet for 160 million years. They consumed the vegetation of tall trees and, as some modern species still do, they swallowed stones to break down the plant matter they ate.

Petrified remains of ostrich-like dinosaurs called ornithomimosauria, which were first discovered in 1964, are scattered on the ground. Their skulls were lightly constructed – more like the moa than today's ostrich – their toothless jaws shaped like spatulas.

I have become disorientated. My footsteps don't exist. I find a shadow tattooed in a small cranny and draw my legs up into my chest. A laser of sunlight burns into my knee and it feels like I've been stung by a wasp. My lazy eye runs around a gilded rock face and lands on a bulge that isn't quite in keeping with its composition: a dinosaur egg. In the piercing silence I catch a padded syllable from behind me and find my companions.

Under a stripy, crimson sky, I am surrounded by a petrified forest where the elements have turned the animate into the inanimate. I bend down and pick up a tarbosaurus finger bone from the remains of its shattered skeleton. Tarbosaurus translates appropriately as 'alarming reptile'. Growing to some 14 metres in length and weighing between 2 and 5 tons, it was one of the largest carnivores to have lived on land, looking a bit like a tyrannosaurus rex and just as lethal.

As little as 5 per cent of dinosaur species have been discovered. Petrified mussels lie on the floor, like a child's interrupted game of marbles. In an infinite landscape composed of parched colour, I succumb to the Gobi's power and bow. All life forms have one thing in common: death. Perhaps life is, in itself, a conscious organism: a species, an idea, a living organism, an expression. I like the theory of panspermia – the idea that life does not evolve on one planet alone.

I find Thomas on a crumbling ridge and we sit down on a petrified tree trunk. "Others find petrol," Thomas says.

"What?"

"They meet us somewhere," he replies, pointing into the desert.

"Look," I fumble with the compass hanging around my neck, "I don't want to bother you, but I don't think there's any sign of human life for hundreds of miles, let alone a petrol station. Doesn't this concern you?"

Thomas gazes over the glowing desert. "Maybe, yes." In the waves of the setting, molten sun, I feel irrelevant. "There," he says after twenty minutes, and points some distance below us. "There they are." We scramble down a piste of dinosaur shingle back to a cup of tea.

We're so far into the desert that Naraa calls this place 'the dangerous Gobi'. To the west, the desert goes on and on into nothing, as if it's being sucked into an enormous void beyond the darkening horizon. It looks turbulent and menacing, but how many dinosaur sites remain undiscovered out there and what other secrets? Baba is worried about the weather and we're running out of water and petrol. Dust squalls rake the desert floor and our bus quivers in the grip of savage gusts.

Thomas explains that if it does rain, which is unlikely but possible, the ground beneath us will turn into a quagmire. Naraa looks concerned. Her gutsy grin has been replaced by concerned glances around her and towards the sky. It's time to leave the Gobi, and our valiant white minibus turns north. Thomas informs me that he is planning the next expedition and that we will return again, but with a couple of helicopters in tow.

Some hours later we leave the Gobi behind us, driving through a range of mountains that separates the desert and the steppe, like a wall. We find three gers huddled next to each other, stop for the night and buy a sheep which is killed with a small incision into its chest, severing the aorta. The process looks more humane than the Kazakhs' approach.

The following day we drive through the night and when we arrive at UB in the early hours of the morning, Baba looks a bit jaded.

– Chapter 9 –

In Stein's footsteps

I've read several books about the Taklamakan Desert and its role in the old Silk Road. It sounds isolated, hostile and far from civilisation's clutches. In a world atlas the Taklamakan looks like an enormous blank in western China, as if the cartographer took one look at it and decided to leave it till later. Closed to the world since 1930, barred and padlocked, the south Taklamakan track has recently been opened where some of the ancient Silk Road settlements remain forgotten and preserved. The thought of lost desert towns and dwellings is too much to resist.

At the end of August I catch a train from UB and snake my way on a collection of trains out of Mongolia, into China's arid Inner Mongolia and onto Beijing. Boiled and burnt goat heads are shoved through the train windows as a substitute for the more acceptable Mars bars and Coca-Cola. A firing range of phlegm and urine awaits any passenger who, like me, might stick their head unwittingly out of the window. A Chinese man falls asleep on my back and others goggle. I arrive in Beijing to find it preparing for the nation's fiftieth anniversary.

When I check into a small hotel close to the Forbidden City I'm given a room beneath street level. Out of the top of the window I can see legs and bicycle tyres, and the room is pestered by the gagged clacking and clanging of carts. Twenty-nine years old in a gloomy room smelling of mouldy

carpets. Budget travelling is bad for my health and birthdays remind me of my mortality with a ferocious belligerence.

Saturn Return is the term astrologers use for the years between twenty-eight and thirty-two, particularly the twenty-ninth year. They describe it is an astrological passage of rites, marking the end of youth and the beginning of the productive adult years. They teach that each of us is challenged to take responsibility for our own journey and begin to give expression to a unique voice that comes from within. It is the culmination of a thirty-year evolutionary process, a complete cycle spanning the entire life to that point.

If you've been working towards what's right for you, these years of Saturn Return can be a period of reward, but if you're not pursuing a life true to yourself, this can be a time of change, self-analysis and consolidation. It is a pruning of the individual, an unsettling period when the conscious and unconscious dispose of all detritus that is not relevant to the crux of your human essence, such as inappropriate ideas, objects and people. If lessons are not learned or confronted during the first Saturn Return, astrologists predict the same problems will return during the second Saturn Return at the age of fifty-eight.

Not wanting to pass the evening alone, I hail a cab to a bar called Huxley's, which is frequented by expats. I order a pint of lager and talk to a couple of English brothers in their mid-twenties who explain that they're involved in commercial real estate. They buy me a drink. I tell them about the Gobi and that I saw lots of dinosaur bones. Their eyes widen, as if in disbelief. "What were you on?" one of them says. They laugh in that raucous way that only people who've been to public school can do. "Another drink?" They're being very generous, and a few pints later I climb into a cab and return to my dark hotel room.

The next afternoon I board a plane and fly over 1500 miles to Urmuchi, on the other side of China. The desert beneath us looks like a sandy sea, only sometimes interrupt-

ed by a range of spiny mountains. Urmuchi is the capital city of Xinjiang, a province the size of Outer Mongolia which has forty-four ethnic minorities residing within its boundaries. The Uighurs are dominant in this area. They established a kingdom in northern Mongolia in the eighth century, but were kicked out 100 years later where they settled in the Turpan region, to be again expelled by the Mongolians in the thirteenth century, and thereafter created their own culture among the Taklamakan oases.

It was the Uighurs who, before Buddhism, most likely introduced the singing bowls to the Asian continent. Conceived from the science of sound and vibration, they were used for healing. They were made from a consecrated alloy containing precious and semi-precious stones and components of meteorite. Tibetan Buddhism places the origin of the bowls in their culture with the Bonpo of pre-Buddhist Tibet who, according to cultural records, originated in the Himalayas 18,000 years ago. A Bonpo is a practitioner of Bon, meaning 'to call', and Bonpo translates as 'reciting magical formulas'. This culture was developed by Tonpo Shenrab Miwoche who collated the shamanic practices and outlawed all animal sacrifices. Geographically, it is perhaps no coincidence that the Indian Sanskrit word 'Shamballa' is used to describe the kingdom of ZhangZhu, the spiritual home of the Bonpo.

We land and I take a cab into Urmuchi. It is difficult to be complimentary about this hotchpotch of a city surrounded by torrid desert and steaming rocks. It is an unattractive, insalubrious conurbation in pursuit of its identity, where twentieth-century architecture competes with ancient mud abodes signatured with sore-infested donkeys. I check into a hotel and go to a restaurant where menus are hand-picked from plastic boxes containing live snakes, frogs and a variety of other slithering unknowns. It's too hot to be adventurous, so I settle for a bowl of noodles.

I take a bus through the desert to Turpan, south of Urmuchi which is situated in the world's lowest depression, some 426 feet below sea level. The heat is beyond torpid. It immobilises the mind and body, so that all you want to do is lie under a tree with a glass of ice-cold lemonade. At night the sheets are too warm to lie on, as temperatures of 42°C refuse to abate. There's not a breath of air and in a futile effort to cool down, I run a bath of cold water. Side-streets are canopied with vines and healthy-looking donkeys pull rickety carts. People without legs push themselves along the ground on wheels attached to planks of wood, and lepers covered in filthy sheets have teamed up with other disfigured and limbless individuals to haunt the entrance of the marketplace.

I visit a couple of ruined settlements outside Turpan, but they're filled with signposts and tourists. This is not the Silk Road I hoped to find. I return to Urmuchi on a bus that breaks down, so some of the Uighurs and I go for a swim in a desert stream. I wave down another crowded bus and sit on the floor, where the Uighurs touch my hair and stroke my skin, somewhere between curiosity and boredom.

I arrive back in Urmuchi and walk into the offices of the CITS (Chinese International Travel Service), the state-controlled tourist operator. I ask a short man with tousled hair about the ancient settlements on the southern fork of the old Silk Road. He removes a map and with the back of a pencil indicates a few of the old sites around Khotan. "Few people go there," he says, and tells me that there is an overnight bus across the desert to Khotan. If you head east across the desert, the oasis of Khotan is one of only three working towns in over almost 500 miles. "When you get to Khotan," he continues, "there is one of our offices there." He writes down their address on the back of his business card.

I buy a ticket on the sleeper bus and find my allocated top bunk bed. The Uighurs chatter unobtrusively as we drive onto the best bit of tarmac that I've travelled on in Inner Asia to begin our crossing of the desert, heading towards a sinking orange sun.

Baron von Richtofen first employed the term 'Silk Road' to describe the trading route from the then Roman port of Alexandria to the present day city of Xi'an. The Taklamakan, which accounted for a third of its distance, is a desert that inherited the title 'Sea of Death'. In Uighur Taklamakan means 'You go in and you don't come out'. In the late nineteenth and early twentieth century, explorers set out to find the lost cities that were rumoured to exist in the desert: Sven Hedin, Sir Aurel Stein, Albert Von Le Coq, Paul Pelliot and others. Stein removed 30,000 manuscripts from a secret library cave in Dunhuang alone. Both Stein and Hedin passed through Khotan, as did Marco Polo 600 years before.

I wake up the following morning to find that we've crossed the desert. I slept through it and now we're 370 miles south of Urmuchi. We've arrived on the south Taklamakan road which threads between the world's second largest desert and the toenails of the Tibetan plateau. It's a region of uninviting geography squiggled with radiation, nuclear weapons and civil unrest. A vast shifting mass of boiling sand dunes and the odd mountain chain.

The entrances into Khotan are policed by the officious Chinese militia, as are most of the smaller oasis villages. There are a million Uighurs living in Khotan and they want their independence. Some have resorted to blowing up establishments in Urmuchi and targeting people for assassination. Barricades are as simple as a few donkeys, carts and cows sewn together with string. Others are more sophisticated, but they all bristle with an assortment of weapons as soldiers study local identity papers at length. Wanted posters have been stuck to the sides of army Jeeps and the terrorists look so young.

The bus drops me outside the only hotel in Khotan and I walk up the steps into the foyer. The hotel feels empty and unused. I am shown to a clean room with a shower, dump my pack on the floor and show the receptionist the

address that I was given. She scribbles a map with a blue biro and I wander out onto an empty, dusty street lined with motionless poplars.

Walking in the leafy, but listless shade, I follow her directions, arriving at the entrance of a grey box-like building where I climb some stairs that emerge onto a long corridor. I find a door that is ajar and explain to a man called Nounai, who speaks English, that I'd like to see one of the old Silk Road settlements. He listens attentively and offers me a chair. "What about Niya?" I ask, a pearl of sweat trickling down my forehead as if someone's stroking me with the nib of a long blade of grass.

"Four thousand dollars," Nounai replies, his willowy frame swivelling to the left as if caught in a breeze.

"Endere?"

"Six thousand dollars. Three days by horse." The words almost whistle through his amber teeth and cracked lips.

"Oh," I answer. My shoes scuff the floor and dust puffs into lines of sunlight, like disturbed sediment in the shallows of a silted pond. My throat is parched and the room smells of baked body sweat. "And Rawak?"

"Few hundred dollars."

"How few?" I lean forward to catch a fragment of moving air from an old, clucking fan.

"Three hundred."

"Two hundred."

"Two ninety."

"Two ten."

"Two ninety. Final." Nounai's eye fissures twitch. With a bony finger he removes a flake of crispy, brown snot from his left nostril.

"Okay." He examines the flake that is sitting on the ball of his right little finger and places it in his mouth. Deal completed. "I'll organise Jeep," Nounai says. "Now lunch." Nounai is Han Chinese. The Han dynasty established their culture so well that 'Chinese' means a man of Han.

Chinngis Khan wanted to slaughter the Han Chinese, the lot of them, to make room for the horses needed for his expanding army, but his advisers considered this a trifle harsh and counselled him against the idea.

Rawak is a Buddhist stupa constructed 1500 years ago and was inhabited for over 1000. The explorer Stein first visited the site in 1901 and in his book, *The Ruins of Desert Cathay*, he writes of

> *the total absence of land marks. The cloudy sky, so rare in the region. I sighted once more the white brick pile of the ruined stupa of Rawak ...*
>
> *My thoughts had dwelt often on this imposing old ruin, and the fine series of sculptures brought to light by my excavations in 1901. The preserved colossal statue of the shrine was now almost completely hidden under the ridge of sand some six metres high. Of the south-east face too, less emerged from the sand than before, yet enough to show me the destruction which had been dealt by the hand of man since my visit. My care in burying these again under the sand, just as I found them proved in vain.*

An Uighur comes up to me while I'm waiting for Nounai at the entrance to the bazaar. His skin is the colour of tan enamel and under the rim of a purple skull hat, spotted with white dots, his pale chestnut eyes flutter across my face. "NATO help?" he stammers hastily. I cough uncomfortably, and he melts into the bazaar.

I follow Nounai to a table under the bazaar's awnings and ease myself into a torn, but clean sofa. A barefooted azure-eyed Caucasian adolescent swaddled in Muslim clothes stands outside her stall. I smile at her and she returns a smile larger than life, before blushing and swiftly covering her mouth with a veil, as a man gently glares at her. The bazaar looks like a huge banqueting hall. Tables are lavishly laid with a variety of dishes and platters as families dine. The air is a blend of cut vegetables, incense and charred fat. There's a

crowd, but no jostling, or squabbling, and through the arch at the end, under decorated wooden trellising, I can see the shimmering figures of crouched and bent pedlars. I pick at some rice and chicken. "How far is Rawak?"

"An hour by Jeep and two hours by foot," Nounai mumbles between chopsticks, piled with food. "I've organised guide and a person from museum to go."

"Why the museum?"

"Authorities insist."

"How many foreigners have been there?"

"Maybe ten," Nounai answers.

"And Endere?"

"Someone went there three years ago."

"Is it possible to go from Khotan, to Endere, to Niya?"

He looks confused. "Someone's already done that."

"Who?"

"Stein."

The idea that these sites have been visited by only a handful of outsiders since the days of Marco Polo, saturates my mind with excitement. It seems that I've been born into the wrong age.

The Silk Road was a variety of commercial routes connecting Europe with the Far East by land and sea. They came into being around 200 BC and continued as trading arteries until AD 900, a time span that encompassed the peaks of both the Roman and Chinese empires. Silk was the most valuable, if not the most commonly traded, commodity. In the days of the Silk Road, merchants moving west from Xi'an would have travelled to the Jade Gate at Yumen along well-constructed roads under the supervision of watchtowers and walls. The Jade Gate served as a vague frontier between China and the west. Beyond this point the road became precarious as it strayed into the untamed wilds of the 'barbarian lands' towards the oasis town of Dunhuang.

This settlement served as a staging post for travellers going into, and coming out of, the Lop and Taklamakan

deserts. From Dunhuang the routes forked around the Taklamakan in northern and southern branches. The northern road passed by Hami, Turpan, Kizil and Kucha, before merging with Kashgar. The southern trail went through Loulan, Niya and Khotan. The nature of the desert often determined which road the traveller would take.

Storms, drifting sands and desert marauders, all of which are real threats today, often made travel impossible for even the most experienced caravans. As one eighth-century traveller noted, 'in some places one merely followed the bleached bones of previous unwary travellers as a guide, without knowing whether one was on the correct path'. The Bactarian camel was the primary form of transport in the desert and remains the preferred choice of today's desert dwellers. It can locate water several miles away and is able to sense subtle changes in the desert's temperament which portend storms.

Silk left China in a partially worked state, reeled from silkworms' cocoons into wholesale spools. It was taken to Parthia and Palmyra where the silk was dyed and set into bolts for onward shipment to Rome. Such was its popularity that in the first century AD, Rome forbade men to wear silk as it constituted 'an immoral drain' on the empire's treasury. Silk's secret defied Roman entrepreneurs. Even in the second century AD, they believed that silk grew on trees. Romans purchased spices, silk, coral, pearls, white jade, linen carpets, musical instruments and wool. The Chinese bought glass, metal goods and horses that were much bigger than their native ponies.

Few traders travelled from Rome to China. A merchant might purchase some carpets in one oasis and exchange them for white jade in another before finally purchasing a quantity of silk.

Khotan disappears into a dusty track lined with regimented avenues of poplar trees and the leaves rustle as if whispering a song of a distant sea. The last tree falls away

behind us and we are quickly surrounded by an eternity of undulating sand. There is no trail and the sky becomes patchy grey. There is nothing ahead of us, or around us, except the desert and the odd withered, gangly or spiky weed.

Two thin, bronzed, elderly Uighurs emerge from a gully between sand dunes leading donkeys laden with scorched tamarisk branches. My guide mutters and shrugs his shoulders. The elderly Uighur replies, raises his arm and points into the glaring desert. Okay, Rawak's over there somewhere. We drive around a large sand dune and park the Jeep.

"Do you know where Rawak is?" I ask.

The guide looks at me, knowing he's been rumbled. "Gphh," he snuffles. "Emm. No."

"Do any of you know?"

"Museum man here last year," he stutters with a wispy smile.

We walk into the desert, traversing one sand dune after another as the sky darkens. A small brown snake wriggles away in front of me and I grasp a water bottle in one hand, my sketchbook in the other as we veer around a towering crescent dune. Two hours later the ground in front of us is strewn with pottery fragments in a depression that might once have been a pond. Rawak's surreal, stubby head pokes behind a dune, like a chimney. I scramble up the dune, sand dribbling away under my feet, to see this ancient stupa in its entirety. It looks like a listing ship struggling to stay afloat.

The north, west and east walls have been all but consumed by the sands and pottery fragments lie around as if smashed last week. I kneel down and rummage through the debris, letting fistfuls of sand run through my fingers. Turning over an ancient green coin in my hand, I scour the ground. There are a couple of old tins, perhaps evidence of Stein's expedition. The stinging silence has returned and mountains of sand race around me. The stupa itself appears to have once harboured rooms, but these have been engulfed by the desert.

"Hey," my guide shouts. "Come. Look." I join my three companions, who are scraping sand away from an interior wall. A painted forehead, an angry eye, a finger, a hand, an arm. "Buddhist frescos," he wheezes, scrabbling in the sand. I kneel down and pull handfuls of sand away. Between the four of us we uncover parts of four life-size figures and figurines. It looks as if these paintings cover the inner wall, so there must be more inside the stupa. This place needs a professional dig. It's just as I've imagined finding a lost city as we reveal more corroded paintings and, with each scoop of sand, Rawak springs into life.

"Here," my guide calls, his head protruding from behind a parapet. "Come here." We shift sand and rubble away from a notch of the eastern wall: a statue, and another. It's like unwrapping presents. The museum man taps my elbow and crumples his lips, pointing to a life-size decapitated bust. The museum man says something. "Head stolen since last year," my guide translates. They look concerned, not so much for that theft as for Rawak's survival. I suppose this is the case for many of the lost Taklamakan cities. Paintings inside, statues outside, Rawak must have been quite something. It still is. The sky is becoming increasingly stormy and the wind is throwing up sand around us. We've got to get out of here. We bury our finds in the sand and walk into the desert's maw.

Only a few steps into our return journey, Rawak becomes invisible in a swirling blizzard of sand. We're two hours by foot into the world's worst desert. I wrap my sarong around my face and sand bites into my legs. I can't see more than a few yards as the wind conjures up whirling columns of sand and I bend my head into my chest. Footprints don't exist and, clasping the compass around my neck, I curse myself for having left my GPS and maps at the hotel. The Chinese don't take kindly to such equipment in areas like the Taklamakan. I'm only encouraged by the resolve of the plucky museum man who is slightly younger than me. Sven Hedin's first expedition into the Taklamakan

in February 1895 ran out of water and they got lost shortly after their departure. Only Hedin and one Uighur returned. The other three Uighurs died in the desert.

We lumber through clouds of sand and find ourselves in another pottery-littered site with some foundations stamped into the ground. "Not many people know about this place," my guide says. I look at him in a frenzy of concern, and then at the swarming sand. We did not come this way, but the museum man seems reassured by these ruins. I watch him point optimistically, and with some purpose, at a ridge of sand dunes. Sand spirals and twists and the astringent wind changes the formation of the dunes before my eyes. My companion heads off in the opposite direction to which he's pointed. In a moment of undisciplined panic I catch his attention, raise my arm and point into the desert: "I think the Jeep's over there." He looks puzzled and I can see in his eyes that he isn't sure of his route. The driver and my guide, having no idea where we are, stand silently as the sand blows around us and I quickly realise my extreme stupidity. His judgment has to be better than mine in this 'You go in and don't come out' desert. I shake my head, smile and with my hands tell him to ignore my observations.

We walk on and on, up and over sand dunes as the desert looks increasingly like a stormy, muddy sea. I laser onto the body language of the museum man as each time he reaches the peak of a sandy ridge, he stops, looks around, then doggedly strides off. It's proving to be a barometer to our situation. His pace quickens and he breaks into a run. So do I. And there, revealed on the other side of a dune, is our Jeep. He grins, but his eyes appear bloodshot with anxiety. I return a large smile. "Well done." Turning to my 'guide' I say, "Will you ask him if he was worried about getting back?"

"He says, yes."

Heading back to Khotan we drive past a few wilting, scraggy plants and the closer we get to the oasis, the grey skies turn blue again.

– Chapter 10 –

The Taklamakan to the Tibetan plateau

A man with almond eyes slides into a chair next to me, then looks over his shoulder. "I'm being followed by the Chinese," he says furtively.

"What?" I reply.

"Secret police. You must follow me. Two minutes after I leave, turn left ... tree ... right ... street."

"Where am I meeting you?"

He gets up and walks out of the Khotan hotel lobby. I arranged to meet this man to buy antiques, not get apprehended by the authorities. I watch a reedy Chinese man with sallow skin, shiny black hair and sunken eyes fold up his paper, follow him to the steps at a discreet distance and sneak outside into the dusk. I linger in the lobby and then leave. Left. Right. What tree? Street. I retrace my steps. I try another left and right. Two minutes has become twenty and I've no idea where my man's got to. I turn around and see the Uighur cycling towards me. He stops and asks, "What happened?"

"Got lost, sorry."

"Follow me."

He seems used to playing cat and mouse as we walk down a shady side-street. I feel as if I'm part of a thriller as we stop outside a door, knock and the door is cautiously opened. We step into a courtyard where a man is praying in Muslim fashion next to a lantern under coloured eaves. I'm led into a small room where I sit down on a long sofa. The

Uighur disappears and returns with another man who looks tense. Both have plump sacks slung over their shoulders. They sit either side of me and garnish the table with antiques: bracelets, pottery, bangles, ancient coins and oil lamps, copper pouring vessels stained green, old mulberry bank notes, rings, statuettes, Roman- and Greek-looking antiquities, and a variety of articles I've never seen before.

"Where do you get this stuff from?"

"Some from the desert. The rest I buy at bazaars."

The objects glisten in the candlelight and we're interrupted by a wadded patter of feet across the courtyard. The light is extinguished. He holds my elbow and whispers, "Shhhh." The other Uighur leaves the room to investigate, then returns with a smile. They remove tattered embroidered fabrics which seem to be fragments of scarves, or wall hangings. "These were found at Niya and Endere. Two thousand dollars."

"My budget goes to about forty dollars."

He looks bewildered. "No problem." He carefully folds the fabrics up as if they might disintegrate, places them between cardboard and wraps them in newspaper, while I trawl through the remnants of the Silk Road's treasure. I select two coins which appear different from others I've seen, a tiny Roman copper amphora and an ancient white engraved jade oil lamp.

He looks at the two coins I've chosen and shakes his head. "I've only ever found three of them. No one knows where they come from, or how old they are. I want to keep them." I look momentarily glum, theatrically so, then he agrees to let me have one. Is this stubby verdigris coin in my right palm perhaps evidence of the Agharti Nicholas Roerich speaks of in the Altai? In his book *Shambhala* Roerich writes:

And again when we approached Khotan the hoofs of our horses sounded hollow as though we rode above caves and hollows. Our caravan people called to our attention saying,

'Do you hear what hollow subterranean passages we are crossing? Through these passages, people who are familiar with them can reach far off countries.' When we saw entrances of caves, our caravaners told us, 'Long ago people lived there; now they have gone inside; they have found a subterranean passage to the subterranean kingdom. Only rarely do some of them appear on earth. At our bazaars such people come with strange, very ancient money, but nobody can remember a time when such money was in usage here.'

On the way back to the hotel I am overcome with an explosive pain in my bowels. I have about thirty seconds. I run to the darkest shadow under a poplar and yank my shorts to my knees. Just in time too.

The next morning I climb onto a bus. The tyres are bald, nuts and bolts tremble, rubber dangles from the ceiling and the engine hisses as we set off east. The desert is flat and bereft of life. The track, if that's what it can be called, has in places been obliterated by flash floods, until eventually it disappears altogether and so begins the first of many stops as the bus gets bogged down in the sand.

Everyone gets out, pats the sand in front of the bus with their feet, like spectators at a polo match between chukkers. Long wooden poles are placed under the tyres, the driver starts the engine and we push. The bus lurches into life and everyone cheers. An hour later, we get stuck again and the process is repeated until, some twenty-four hours later, we arrive at the bus's terminus, the oasis town of Chiemu.

We clamber out and I ask a bus official the departure time of the bus to Charklik. She shrugs her shoulders. I try again, until I'm able to determine that no one has any idea when the bus is leaving, because it hasn't returned from Charklik. It's six days overdue. I have fourteen days left on my visa and I'm stranded at a desert oasis. I check into a surprisingly comfortable hotel which seems to have an abundance of military personnel and slip into a daily routine.

I get up, breakfast on stodgy dumplings and green tea, go to the bus station where the official shrugs her shoulders. I walk out of the town through avenues of poplars, past mud homes trellised by vines with fat, droopy leaves, where black pigs and white goats slumber. I cross the muddy river, walk into the desert and sit on top of a large dune, surveying the oasis. On the sixth morning the official beams at me. The bus is leaving in an hour. I check out of the hotel, grab my pack and climb onto a bus that looks distressed and is crowded with Uighurs.

Another very uncomfortable journey starts as we drive into the desert and the oasis disappears into the haze. More and more the desert looks as if it's been churned, grilled, sandpapered and finally varnished. Waves of shaded, yellow sand dunes peel away beside us. We haven't seen any other human life for nine hours. For four of them a boy's been gaping at me, jammed in between boxes, baskets and sacks. I lost my Walkman to Uighurs some hours ago and watch it rotate around the passengers.

We're 370 miles east of Khotan. My shirt's drenched with sweat and sticks to the back of the tiny metal seat. A hand appears by my elbow with a slice of honey melon. The orange flesh is petalled with juice and I hold it against my parched lips. I bite into the soft, crunchy centre and the fruit evaporates in my mouth.

We cross a dried up riverbed, then we all get out to watch the driver reverse for a run-up. The engine chokes, water pours into the sand and the bus dies at the foot of the bank. The sun sinks into the desert and the sky turns turquoise, then indigo. The fan belt is broken, the gear-box has collapsed and the exhaust pipe snapped in two. Indigo becomes desert black and the sky sparkles. Our driver throws his head back, screams, covers his face with grimy hands, as if pleading to a spirit and chants a sonorous, "*Yaiayaiayiayia ...*" before ending with a piercing "*Mama*". The insouciant Uighurs chuckle, the sand smiles and I walk

off to find some wood. A stout man builds a fire and settling myself away from the others because I don't feel I belong with them, I fall asleep to their throaty singing.

Blackness. Flashing lights. *Puk puk puk puk puk puk puk*, like early morning Greek fishing boats. A smell of charcoal. Desert Gypsies. Babbling and laughing, they pull and push carts which are harnessed to engines mounted on wheels. My fellow travellers are silent. I detect curled lips and sultry sneers, as if these Gypsies are somehow tarnished. They make their camp away from us, build fires and huddle around the flames.

The bus roars into life and peering through drowsy, squinting eyes, I feel like an actor on a stage caught in its headlights. The Uighurs stand up sleepily and stretch their arms under a dazzling inky sky. A man is folded up asleep on the ground and an Uighur kicks him in the small of his back. Galvanised, the man leaps into the air, runs into the desert and comes to an abrupt halt. The Uighurs laugh. We push the bus and an aged woman sitting on the ground sucking on some honey melon flaps her hands at me. I stop pushing, smile at her and hoarsely reply, "Why don't you come and help us, you toothless crone?" She smiles back. A couple of hours later our bus arrives at a tiny oasis and we park in a courtyard. The driver looks raddled.

I wake up early and saunter into a leafy courtyard, past the parked bus and step onto the dusty, sandy track. The air smells of feathery green leaves and the sunlight is warm, so that you can tilt your head to one side and bask in it. There are some mud houses the colour of faded sepia and if you stand on the track, you can see poplars running off in both directions into the yellow desert. A stream moves lazily under a bridge and a small fish wags its body behind a clump of silky, cabbage green weed. This is how oasis villages should be and I don't even know the name of it. It's not marked on my map.

I walk to the opposite side of the track and into the open doors of a tiny convenience store, which appears to

double as the village restaurant. I point to a pair of chopsticks. An old woman with hoary hair and brown, crinkly skin, nods her head in acknowledgment, then grins, inadvertently displaying her few stained teeth. I sit outside and a few minutes later a bowl of noodles with spring onions and cloves of raw garlic in soya sauce is presented to me.

The relationship with one's fellow passengers traversing the desert on a clapped-out bus is perhaps not dissimilar to an ocean crossing on a small, dilapidated ship. Much is said with a smile and a look. We board the bus and the oasis vanishes into the desert behind us. The sand dunes have been replaced by a shimmering, flat, stony scenery.

Some hours later we arrive in the outskirts of Charklik on the Taklamakan's eastern boundary. Charklik is not an attractive place. It feels abandoned and the buildings are ugly. The surrounding desert looks like a steaming frying pan and the Uighurs have all but disappeared. I feel as if I'm back in Han China. I book myself into the only hotel I can find and make inquiries about onward travel. The main track out of here is north via Korla, Turpan and Hami, but I want to punch east through the mountains to Dunhuang. Not only is it a shorter route, but I don't want to retrace my direction to Turpan. There appears to be one bus which goes east via a desert path, but as a foreigner I'm forbidden to travel that route. I step into a concrete building and walk into a communist-style office where a bored Chinese official, his expression moulded by indifference, is sitting behind an empty desk. I ask him if I can hire a Jeep.

"It really is borderland territory beyond here," he drones.

"What do you mean?"

"Lawless. We can't take responsibility." His skin is a pasty yellow, his brown eyes impassive.

"Oh." I feel intimidated as he rolls a pen around the desk.

"Jeep hire is thousand dollars."

"I can't afford that. Three hundred?"

"One thousand," he replies curtly.

A slim Chinese woman with lacquered black hair follows me outside where a soldier, his face covered with a cap, is sprawled over a hammock strung up between two poplar trees. "Where are you going?" she enquires in pellucid English.

"Beijing."

"Beijing," she says softly, as though it's a magical story-book place. A child dressed in a blue boiler suit stops, tilts his head, squats and through the slit in his trousers, shits on the side of the road. He gets up and walks off, much like a dog. "Beijing. Beijing," she quietly echoes. "Beijing."

"Just enjoy it," a Vietnamese-looking man says to me.

"What?" I've never seen this man before but maybe my face is a portrait of rumpled frustration. Time and cash are running out and the year is unfurling towards winter.

"Why do you want to take that road?" he asks, with a genuine look of concern.

"Because it's difficult," I say stubbornly.

"The road to Tibet is difficult too."

"What?"

"The road to Tibet is hard," he says, and walks away.

I'm losing it, or am I?

A fidgety man dressed in an old army uniform agrees to take me beyond the borderlands for a few hundred dollars. He has eyes like pins and speaks in a monotone. We drive through the desert's last dregs and weave up and up, into stark, jagged mountains. The desert, a tablet of shimmering ochre, disappears behind us as we crawl along a riverbed through a narrow gorge. The Jeep stalls, starts and stops. The distances between the starts and stops diminish to a few yards. The Jeep stops. The driver scrambles out, removes an oily cloth from his pocket and pokes frothing plugs, steaming tubes and whining cylinders. I watch his stunted hands jab at a spewing cap, then mop his brow.

The mountains look desolate, sheened with a stillness that's almost empty. When a blue truck comes up behind us I lurch for my pack and wave it down. I turn to the Jeep driv-

er, who shakes his head and motions that he can repair the engine. Happy in the thought that more vehicles will pass, I wave them on and watch the truck coil up into the mountains, emerging and disappearing, as it ducks in and out of the contours. The driver looks chuffed and closes the bonnet. Our Jeep speeds off for a mile or so, sneezes and then dies. Six hours later there has been no passing traffic. Zilch.

In Urmuchi and Khotan I was told that bandits work this area. Is this part of a plot? Is my driver in league with these bandits, or perhaps the Uighur terrorists? Will I be carted off? Ransomed? Killed? It will be dark in a few hours and then what? We're in the middle of another wilderness nearly 10,000 feet up. I reach for my Leatherman knife and find its presence oddly reassuring as I leave the driver wrestling with the engine and walk up the winding track.

A few hours later, as the last pencilled pink rays vanish from the satin mountain ridges, I'm growling in the back of the Jeep. Then I look up to see balls of fire, yellow flames, the bonnet and windscreen engulfed. My driver's running away and I recoil out of the Jeep to sprint in the opposite direction. The front of the Jeep resembles a bonfire, billowing black smoke. When I stop to look back flames are sprouting from the roof. The air reeks of burnt rubber and burning oil.

I run back for my pack and, deciding the Jeep's not going to blow up, crab-walk to the back seat and pull it out. The driver decides that he, too, will make a bid for something and removes the two jerry cans of petrol. We look at each other and watch the flames subside, then examine the engine. It's black and smoking. We haven't seen a vehicle for nine hours and now, as if planned, a white car with six Chinese squashed into it drives up next to us.

My renegade chauffeur talks to them and then turns to me, flicking through the pages of my pocket Mandarin dictionary. He points to, repair, Jeep, wait, then raises a greasy finger at me. "No way." I pick up my pack and clamber over

four Chinese into the car's boot. My driver squeezes into the front seat and cringes at the sight of his burnt-out Jeep as we drive off.

We arrive in a small mining town enshrouded in a smog of white dust and I am shown into a small dormitory. I sit on a bed in the dark until a man flashes a torch in my face and holds it there. "Get that fucking torch out of my eyes," I snarl.

The next morning I buy a honey melon, and climb onto a small bus with fabric seats and air-conditioning. The Chinese point at the melon sitting in my lap. For the last two weeks it's been a necessity and now it's a novelty. I'm out of the desert and the borderlands, back into administrative China. The night bus is taking me to Dunhuang. To check that we're going in the right direction I look out of the window and find the north star between the Big Dipper and Cassiopeia.

Dunhuang is primed for tourism and I already miss the Uighurs. I visit the Buddhist grottos where Stein extracted 30,000 manuscripts from a monk for the princely sum of a silver coin. The place is a heaving mass of sweating bodies, moving from one painted cave to another. Many of the grottos are sealed with metal doors and padlocks. I transfer to an overnight train to Lanzhou and catch a bus to the Tibetan Plateau which winds its way up past the wrecks of jeeps, cars and a smouldering bus.

Xiahe, cradled in a mountain basin in Gansu, is the largest Buddhist monastery after Lhasa. A man walks past with a black hole in his face where his nose should be, eaten away by either leprosy or syphilis. Confronted by lines of cloistered prayer wheels I stop as a lama walks past with two bald child apprentices in tow, one of them tripping over his dragging fuchsia robe.

"Alstar."

I spin around and gape at a Tibetan boy of perhaps seven dressed in blue jeans, a T-shirt and a baseball cap. He's

standing next to another boy who seems to be about ten. The younger child stares at me. "What? Alistair?" I ask, dazed and subservient.

"Alstar," he replies cryptically. He looks at me with his brown eyes and, taking my arm, directs me to the inside of a chamber containing a large, colourfully patterned prayer wheel, where he gestures to indicate what I should do. I obey and walk around the wheel three times in a clockwise direction, turning it as I go in the manner suggested. I leave the wheel and walk back into the sunlight, curious to see if the child is still there. The ten-year-old is leaning against the wall, but my guide has vanished. I check the empty side-streets. Nothing. I cannot have been gone for more than three minutes.

I sit down at a table in a café opposite a woman in her thirties with long, mousy hair and order some noodles. "Sam," she says, in an Australian accent.

"No. Alistair."

"No. I mean I'm Sam," she grins. "Where've you come from?"

"The Taklamakan."

"How was it?"

"Lost settlements," I say. "My jeep blew up – stuff like that. And you?"

"I stay here every year. I'm a Buddhist and talk to travellers about it." I tell her about the boy and her blue eyes ignite into life as she exclaims, "Well done."

"What do you mean?"

"Just, well done."

"Okay."

I have no idea what she means, but it sounds nice. I explain that I'm sure I was followed across the desert. I felt it, in the same way that, when I was robbed once, I knew they were going to do it the moment I saw them. There was a jaunty Chinese man who fell over himself to ensure that I knew what was going on between Khotan and Chiemu, yet

when I asked him why he was going to Chiemu, he replied that he was catching a plane. The airport in Chiemu had been shut down two years ago. I checked when I got there.

"My activities are reported," Sam says. "That guy keeps tabs on me." She glances to the left at a sleek man sitting at a table reading a book. "The first time I was told that I was being followed because of my work, I didn't believe it. It's not uncommon for the Chinese to watch foreigners." Four swarthy Tibetan herdsman walk in, their eyes sparkling with the look of the wilderness. They are mostly Mongol in physical build and character, but taller and with longer faces.

I recount a list of peculiar occurrences that started with the reedy man who followed the antiques dealer in Khotan. Then when I went for my strolls into the desert outside the oasis of Chiemu, a soldier would appear and leave when I returned a few hours later. And when I sketched an elderly Uighur who invited me into his house in Chiemu, the following day everything was boarded up, as if the place had been deserted for years. For the previous four days I'd passed his home it was filled with people and animals.

"You've got to watch out for that," Sam replies. "In Tibet tourists introduce themselves to local families who welcome them into their homes, but after they leave the authorities take them in for questioning." I wince. "Don't worry about it," she says, trying to appease my concern. "You're a westerner and you were travelling in a politically sensitive area. It sounds as if they were keeping an eye open, to make sure you made it across the desert."

On the plane back to Beijing I'm handed a copy of *China Daily*. The front page mentions that surveying by foreigners needs stricter regulation. People have been conducting mapping and surveying activities while working on other projects such as construction, tourism, exploration and archaeology. They take along advanced surveying and mapping instruments, including GPS. If foreigners involved in

surveying and mapping in China are not strictly regulated military, economic and other secrets might be stolen.

Beijing is muggy. Not wanting the hassle of having to find a new hotel, I go to the one I stayed in before my departure for Urmuchi and am given the same dank room. I'm too tired to argue. I have a quick bath, catch a cab, find an Irish pub and order a pint of Kilkenny's. With anticipation I watch the condensation collect around the glass as it's poured out. I look at it for a second, then gulp it down in one.

The capital is busy. If you're not worrying about being run over by a car, or flattened by bicycles when crossing a road, then you're plotting a route through the crowd. The Forbidden City and the Summer Palace are crammed with people. There are no still pockets, no empty rooms, no quiet places in the gardens, just people wherever you look and tour groups shuffling behind each other, like herds of cows. I dine in a small restaurant where I order egg rice, lemon chicken, sweet and sour pork and steamed spinach. A man gobs onto the floor next to me and a waitress cleans it up. Another man is so intoxicated that two waiters carry him outside and lift him onto a donkey cart.

Before I came to China twenty-nine days ago, I decided that I would return to UB. I catch the Trans-Mongolian, store my pack under the bottom bunk and climb onto the top bed as the train slides out of Beijing. We arrive at the border at 11 pm. With only half an hour left on my thirty-day visa the Chinese authorities stamp my passport. The carriages are taken off the tracks and replaced onto Mongolian rails: we have officially left China but many people, including me, walk back into China to have a late supper in town.

The train chugs through no man's land into Mongolia where sombre, pernickety customs officers scrutinise our passports and belongings, as if looking to expose their cursory counterparts. These border examinations go on for some hours, by which time passengers are tired, bleary-eyed

and resigned to interruption. I slide the cabin door shut behind me and sniff the cold, night air as our train glides into Mongolia. The stars glitter and it's not long before we're moving through the Gobi. I nibble on a biscuit and return to the compartment.

Three Mongolians are curled up in sleep as I climb onto my bunk. It's good to be back among these people. I pull a grey blanket over me, peep through the curtain at this uncluttered land that I've come to love and fall asleep. I've travelled nearly 5000 miles in thirty days.

– Chapter 11 –

A land of no strangers

In UB I find a small second-floor apartment behind the parliament building with a kitchen, a sitting room, a bathroom and a bedroom. It overlooks some trees and the leaves are a glowing apricot in the luminous, autumnal light. From the tiny balcony, I can see the undulating mountains of the steppe. I rent a small studio in the park, buy some canvases, oil paints and brushes and begin painting.

I want to draw the human form so go to the art university to see if they can help. I talk to a professor in her thirties who tells me that she's been to London's Tate Gallery. We chat about various artists and I ask her what she thinks of Damien Hurst's formaldehyde exhibits. She looks confused. "The thing is," she answers, "is that we see it all the time on the steppe." She knows a couple of people who might be able to model and I leave her my phone number. I stroll to Millie's to have brunch.

"You know who's just left?" Daniel, the manager, says excitedly.

"Who?" I reply.

"Madonna."

"You mean Julia Roberts. She's in town doing a documentary."

"Cool. Julia Roberts. Yeah? She sat there," he says, pointing to a small, round table by the wall. "She flicked through a magazine and ordered a coffee."

I sit down opposite Michael Khone. "How's the *Mongol Messenger*?" I ask. Michael looks at me, or rather over my shoulder. "That's Parrot," he says.

I turn around and see a man dressed in white Arabian garb. "There's no parrot," I reply.

"No," he says, looking at me as if I'm an idiot. "He's called Parrot. He doesn't approve of the way the Mongolian government sells falcons to the Arab sheikhs. He's been kicking up a fuss so the Mongolians threw him in jail for a week to shut him up."

"Anything else?"

"Cattle rustling in the north, outbreaks of the plague and anthrax."

"No scandals then."

"I got a call from the authorities to back off from that murder case I was following."

I tell Michael about the Taklamakan and that I'm now painting. He says he's recently interviewed Mongolia's best artist, Sanchir, and that if I want he can set up a meeting. Parrot gets up and leaves. Without taking his eyes off him, Michael gathers his pen and paper, waits a moment while Parrot disappears down the stairs and slips away after him. A Dutchman in his late twenties sits down at a table next to me and orders a lasagne. "A Mongolian asked me," he says, turning around and taking a sip of his lemonade, "if I wanted to buy a velociraptor skeleton. I thought about it, but it might be difficult to get out of the country."

Three weeks later I arrange to meet with Sanchir. When I arrive at the Ulaanbaatar hotel a bearded European is standing under the entrance. Suddenly, two marble slabs fall either side of him from the overhanging balcony. His body quivers as the hotel doorman rushes out protesting, "Chinese building, Chinese building." I walk into the bar where a pluty-looking man in his fifties, dressed in a dark grey suit and black overcoat, stumbles across the floor to recruit a door handle as a walking prop. His elegant com-

panion, wearing a short black dress, jacket and skimpy blouse, curses under her breath. Her hair is tied into a preened pony-tail and she accelerates past him in the way women reserve for such occasions.

In the corner of the room another Mongolian man projects a neat pile of vomit onto the bench between him and his female friend. The people sitting around the table are unperturbed as he disguises his discharge with a white, paper table napkin. It pauses precariously on top of the warm, festering mound, then slowly disintegrates. Sitting alone at a table drinking an espresso is a man with white hair and beard.

"Sanchir?" I ask. "You look like Hemingway."

"Some say that, others that I look like Lenin. I tell them that I am Sanchir." He strokes his silver beard. I feel as if I'm being analysed. "I love Mongolia. I'm half Polish, but Mongolia is my home. What are you doing here?"

"I woke up with Mongolia in my head."

He stops caressing his beard. "Ahhh, that's different," he says smiling. "I thought your parents sent you." His face and hands are strangely young, as if they belong to a man twenty years his junior. I tell him that I've travelled around Mongolia, recently returned from China and am now painting in UB. "You're an artist?" he asks inquisitively.

"Amateur."

Sanchir visits my studio and examines some nude portraits. "Mongolian women are beautiful. Yes?"

"They're models. That's all."

"You need guidance." He picks up a piece of white chalk and draws a three-dimensional square on the cobalt blue wall. "Start with something simple." He draws a tea cup inside his square. "I was trained at the St Petersburg academy. I think they still teach the old ways." He steals two encouraging glances at one painting of a mother breastfeeding.

"The old ways?"

"Classical. They teach drawing. I visited an artist in Korea," Sanchir says. "He took me to his warehouse. There were large sheets of paper and big tins of paint. He showed me some of his works. Paint splattered and poured onto paper." Sanchir looks unimpressed and gesticulates as if he's emptying a wastepaper basket. "People pay $15,000 for his paintings."

He takes me to his apartment and leads me into a room crammed with drawings and paintings which are stacked on their sides into shelves around the walls. Clumps of clean paintbrushes stick out of jars like bouquets of cotton flowers. There is a large portrait of an aged Mongolian man in the corner and it's as if he's sitting in the room with us. It would seem that good art is uncorrupted by indifference; whole, true and complete, it is perhaps one of the greatest testaments to man's honesty. "The Mongolians will always be nomads," Sanchir says, pensively. "I wouldn't be surprised if they all left UB." He studies me for a moment. "I do not believe in evolution." He fingers his beard. "You should paint." He writes down the details of the academy in St Petersburg. "Remember to be humble as an artist."

A month later ice coruscates on the inside of my apartment's windows. Across the street through the white-decorated web of naked tree fingers I see a brown horse pulling an empty wooden cart, shadowed by a hunched-up figure. Mongolia is frozen and it's the start of one of the harshest winters on record. Already 605,000 animals have died, affecting 100,000 herders, and the government have forecast that a total of 6 million livestock (20 per cent of the national herd) could perish over the next four months. People are starting to die. There are reports of temperatures as low as minus 60°C in Khovsgol and I wonder how the Dukha are bearing up.

I will never know why I woke up with Mongolia and the powerful pull that drew me here. Now, though, it doesn't feel right to stay any longer. Its as if I've spent my time here

living within the books I read in my early schooldays, books about dinosaurs, prehistoric peoples and Marco Polo, possibly looking for something I've lost. This vanished world still exists in Mongolia, perhaps the last bastion of its kind on such a scale. I have found here a pervading sense of release.

Increasingly, the United States and the west look upon the rest of the world as a theme park. What happens if motorways are built through the steppe and tour operators target this sanctuary? What will happen to Mongolia's nomads and their wilderness? I want to put an enormous fence around Mongolia so that it will never disappear, or be lost to the name of progress. The nomadic way of life, pastoral or otherwise, is in our blood. It is an existence that has prevailed for thousands of years and is now threatened, like so many other life forms today. First and second generation Mongolians living in UB have become disillusioned with modern life and are returning to the steppe. Despite government grants to help them, some have lost the ability to survive in the wilderness.

I reach for a fur coat and walk outside. The hairs on the inside of my nose stiffen, almost as if they might chime, and I pull my hat down over my ears. The snow swirls and, when it touches my face, gently reminds me that I'm alive. I walk across the main square, sit down against a Doric column and watch flecks of snow, like fine aluminium shavings, fall out of a night sky.

A long-haired Mongolian walks towards me, flanked by two men. I get up. He stops in front of me. Two of them seize my arms while the third smashes the side of my head and I pass out. I wake up face down in the snow and watch them walk into the blackness. Like veiled demons stalking through a dream, they go in and out of my life in a blurred flash of mystery. Dusting the snow from my clothes I discover they've stolen nothing.

I meet up with Jenya. Two black limousines carrying the Mongolian and Kazakhstan presidents drive up a road lined with policeman wearing fur hats. The only other sign of life, apart from ourselves, is a corpulent Mongolian in a red deel on a horse puffed out in its winter coat.

"Where are we going?" Jenya asks.

"The Institute of Palaeontology. I want to give this champagne to Naraa."

"Naraa? Is that the time when the lama was sitting on the ceiling?"

"No. Dinosaurs."

"I'm going to join the Mormons," Jenya announces.

"I thought you hated missionaries."

"I do, but I can sit around drinking tea all day and then maybe they'll send me abroad."

Two days later I'm told that customs at UB airport have seized my box of personal goods which I organised to be despatched to London. When it passed through the X-ray machine a lump of petrified wood I found in the Gobi apparently looked suspiciously like an old Mongolian tankard. On opening my box they didn't need to rummage far to discover artefacts from the Dukha, the Gobi, the Altai and the Taklamakan, each article carefully packed in a garment of clothing to protect it.

I made a point of smuggling only smaller items, although I dithered about the petrified wood because it was marginally larger than the other objects. I suppose the customs officers must have been bored, or were making a point to a trainee, but whatever the reason they've impounded the lot, except the clothes, which have been forwarded to London. I left a couple of larger dinosaur bones and a Cretaceous turtle with a friend, in the hope not only that I might return one day to collect them, but that she would still be living in UB so they could be retrieved. The others I gave away.

A week later, I receive a call in reply to my advertisement advertising for sale my mini hi-fi and answering machine

(the only specimen I could find in UB). We meet up at Millie's and I agree a price of $300 with an Englishman in his early forties who's recently arrived. When he explains that he's Buddhist I tell him about Xiahe and the boy outside the prayer wheel. He looks genuinely pleased and I feel as if he might be in some way esoterically enlightened.

"Shall I put you on our mailing list?" he offers gently.

"Not now."

"If not now, when?" he replies laconically, but with traces of anxiety in his tone.

I want to say goodbye to Mongolia. I walk up into the surrounding mountains to an ovoo. A white sun hangs in a blue sky and the snow glistens. I pull my shoulders to attention, turn to each of the four points of the compass and bow. "Thank you to the north, thank you to the east, thank you to the south, thank you to the west."

I hoist my pack onto my right shoulder, pull the apartment door shut and step into a waiting cab. We stop outside the station and when I get out to pay the driver with the last of my mutton-smelling tongruks, specks of snow, like tiny particles of polystyrene, roll off my clothing onto the powder beneath me.

There are a few saddled horses parked beside the platform, their heads hung low in the submissive grip of the Mongolian wind. I find my cabin and lie on the top bunk looking out of the window. In a land of no strangers, I have a brand-new set of fingernails, my cigarettes have gone and I've even learnt to burp. Mongolia has let me feel its pulse and touch its heart. The train points south towards China and as it pulls away from the snow-lined platform my eyes became moist.

– Glossary –

airag – the Mongolian name for fermented mare's milk.

beuce – (pronounced beuos) – is a highly coloured fabric that wraps several times around the waist of the deel, always clockwise. It acts primarily as a belt, but is also decorative.

deel – (pronounced del) – traditional Mongolian dress, tailored from neck to ankle, a bit like a large dressing gown. They can be of any colour, but red, blue, green and brown are most common. They vary in depth of wool from season to season.

sain bainuu – Mongolian greeting meaning 'How are you?'

sain ta – reply to above, 'Good'.

sum – a Mongolian provincial capital.

tongruks – Mongolian currency.

– Bibliography –

Allen Benedict. *Edge of Blue Heaven: a journey through Mongolia*, BBC, London, 1998.

Bailey, Alice B. *Ponder on This: a compilation of Alice B. Bailey*, 1978.

Bisch, Jorgen. *Mongolia: unknown land*, Allen & Unwin, London, 1963.

Blackmore, Charles. *The Worst Desert on Earth, crossing the Taklamakan*, John Murray, London, 1995.

Cable, Mildred and Francesca French. *The Gobi Desert*, 1st pub. 1945, Virago, London, 1984.

Crane, George. *Bones of the Master: a Buddhist monk's search for the lost heart of China*, Bantam Press, London, 2000.

Dalrymple, William. *In Xanadu: a quest*, Collins, London, 1989.

Hare, John. *The Lost Camels of Tartary: a quest into forbidden China*, Little Brown, London, 1998.

Hopkirk, Peter. *Foreign Devils on the Silk Road: the search for the lost treasures of Central Asia*, Oxford University Press, Oxford, c.1980.

Humphrey, Caroline. *Shamans and Elders*, Oxford University Press, Oxford, 1996.

Kessler, Adam. *Empires Beyond the Great Wall*, Natural History Museum of Los Angeles, 1993.

Lister, R. P. *Marco Polo's Travels in Xanadu with Kublai Khan*, Gordon & Cremonesi, London, c.1976.

Lovelock, James. *The Ages of Gaia: a new look at life on earth*, Oxford University Press, Oxford, New York, 1982.

Mann, John. *Gobi: tracking the desert*, Weidenfeld & Nicolson, London 1997.

Noble, Christina with Robert Coram. *Bridge Across My Sorrows, the Christina Noble story*, John Murray, London, 1994.

Noble, Christina with Gretta Curran Browne. *Mama Tina: the inspiring sequel to Bridge Across My Sorrows*, John Murray, 1995.

Ossendowski, Ferdinand. *Beasts, Men and Gods*, E.P. Dutton & Co., New York, 1923.

Pfizenmayer, E. W. *Siberian Man and Mammoth*, Blackie and Son, London, 1939.

Polo, Marco (translated by Ronald Latham). *The Travels*, Penguin, London, 1959 edition.

Rinpoche, Sogyal (edited by Patrick Gaffney and Andrew Harvey). *The Tibetan Book of Living and Dying*, Harper San Francisco, c. 1992.

Roerich, Nicholas. *Altai-Himalaya*, Adventures Unlimited Press, Kempton Il., 1929 (2001).

Roerich, Nicholas. *Shambala*, Inner Traditions International, USA, 1930 (revised edition 1990).

Stein, M. A. *Ruins of Desert Cathay: a personal narrative of explorations in Central Asia and Westernmost China*, 2 vols, Macmillan, London, 1912 (reprint 1976).

Stewart, Stanley. *In the Empire of Genghis Khan: a journey among nomads*, HarperCollins, London, 2000.

Tolmachoff, Innokenty P. *The Carcasses of the Mammoth and Rhinoceros Found in the Frozen Ground of Siberia*, American Philosophical Society, Philadelphia.

Wheeler, Alan. *Lords of the Mongolian Taiga*, Department of Central Eurasian Studies, Indiana University, 2000.

World Wide Fund for Nature, *Living Planet Report 2000*.